T0194419

Forty

PROPHETIC POEMS:
SYMBOLIC OF THE GESTATION PERIOD

*Hearing the Voice of God Instilling
Peace during Your Most Difficult Times*

FAY WARREN JARRETT

WESTBOW
PRESS*
A DIVISION OF THOMAS NELSON
& ZONDERVAN

Copyright © 2017 Fay Warren Jarrett.

All rights reserved. No part of this book may be used or reproduced by
any means, graphic, electronic, or mechanical, including photocopying,
recording, taping or by any information storage retrieval system
without the written permission of the author except in the case of
brief quotations embodied in critical articles and reviews.

This book is a work of non-fiction. Unless otherwise noted, the author
and the publisher make no explicit guarantees as to the accuracy of
the information contained in this book and in some cases, names of
people and places have been altered to protect their privacy.

Scripture taken from the King James Version of the Bible.

WestBow Press books may be ordered through booksellers or by contacting:

WestBow Press
A Division of Thomas Nelson & Zondervan
1663 Liberty Drive
Bloomington, IN 47403
www.westbowpress.com
1 (866) 928-1240

Because of the dynamic nature of the Internet, any web addresses or
links contained in this book may have changed since publication and
may no longer be valid. The views expressed in this work are solely those
of the author and do not necessarily reflect the views of the publisher,
and the publisher hereby disclaims any responsibility for them.

Any people depicted in stock imagery provided by Thinkstock are models,
and such images are being used for illustrative purposes only.
Certain stock imagery © Thinkstock.

ISBN: 978-1-9736-0865-3 (sc)
ISBN: 978-1-9736-0866-0 (hc)
ISBN: 978-1-9736-0864-6 (e)

Library of Congress Control Number: 2017917993

Print information available on the last page.

WestBow Press rev. date: 02/22/2018

CONTENTS

INTRODUCTION

What happens to our prayers when we pray? How do God's angels protect us? How do we receive God's favor? How do we develop a determined spirit to always fight, receive the grace to forgive others and ourselves? How do we find the key to pass every test in the spirit, know the signs of Jesus's coming, put a stop to all fears, say yes to God's plans, and recognize the calling of the Prodigal Son to return home? These questions many others are answered in this book as God showed them to me during my difficult times.

God says something new every day, even though God remains changeless. He is same yesterday, today, and forever. But He is also doing a new thing. I am enthusiastic about the new, the freshness. One important thing to note is that God does not view people or circumstances as we do. God takes the worst of us and brings out the best.

> "But God hath chosen the foolish things of the
> world to confound the wise; and God hath chosen
> the weak things of the world to confound the things
> which are mighty." (1 Corinthians 1:27 KJV)

I wrote poems or short verses because they are quick to get to the point. You don't have to read an entire book to know what the chapter is saying as one line of these poems captures the words, emotions, and mind-set of what the Lord wants to say to someone in a particular situation.

These forty prophetic poems, given to me by the Lord, are symbolic of the forty-week gestation period, the time from conception to birth of humans. However, during my writing of these poems, I had no knowledge that this would become a book. All I was doing was listening to the Lord's voice comfort me as I went through a difficult period. However, this was not revealed to me until I wrote the last poem and felt a sense of completion in my spirit. I was destined to write down all these poems as the Lord laid them on my heart. As I lay on my bed, thinking, the Lord revealed to me it was a symbolic of the forty weeks it takes a woman to have a baby. I was surprised because all these poems depicted personal and spiritual issues I was going through during the about eighteen months it took to write them. It was at end of writing all the poems that I realized the organization and layout were miraculously done. After the completion of all forty poems, I also realized the topics they address include fear, praise, worship, success, wisdom, faith, salvation, love, forgiveness, surrender, barrenness, Jesus's coming, determination, encouragement, prayer, angelic protection, and favor.

I often wondered how the Lord could give someone poems to write. Then the Lord assured me that He gave lots of hymns to the churches, and He wants to give poems for His people to use as relief from their worries and to give them inner peace.

These poems are prophetic and revelatory. They are filled with insights and revelations, and they are not just for one reading. You will want to read more than once, as needs and crises arise in your life. If you are having difficulties forgiving someone, read the poem that is for that issue, and listen for God to fill you with inner peace and grace as you open your spirit to the Lord. At the end of each poem, I have added my response.

I have a very quiet personality, but there is a loudness in my spirit that erupts almost uncontrollably, almost effortlessly with praise and adoration for Almighty God, the Creator. He means everything to me and to for our existence, even our very breath, belongs to Him. He strongly pursues you for Himself. No other things or gods must entangle our hearts and defile our love for Him. The quiet heart that will abandon all and give Him full rein will reap the utmost joy and peace. All other things that our fleshy nature seeks—such as health, wealth, and fame—will not be as important as the desire to have Him. To have Him is to have it all in one package. We lack nothing; as the psalmist says, "The Lord is my Shepherd, I shall not want" (Psalm 23:1). This desire to go deeper with Him has opened the way for me to hear the continuous speaking voice of the Lord daily.

I hear the Lord's voice in my everyday situations and struggles. Sometimes He speaks in a calm, loving voice. Sometimes I have visions and dreams. I can't think of a day when God does not speak to me.

My goal is to document some of the life-changing and powerful words that God has given me in my difficult times. It is amazing to know that as I am faced with an issue or situation in my life, the Lord answers me and gives me direction. I find these poems have helped many of my family members. As I read it to them, they immediately got the answer they have sought.

I take absolutely no credit for myself. This is not about me but about a great God, who loves us even when we fail miserably, and He continues to want the best for us.

I don't want to change the exact words for I sense the Lord speaking and directing me as I write. When I first started writing, my plan was to keep the poems for myself. But I felt this unction in my spirit that I would disobey God if others were not able to partake of them.

The words of the poems were given to me for direction, correction, protection, wisdom, growth, and maturity. I have already shared them with close friends and family, but I feel the need to share them with all who may need them. I have seen the power that these poems impart to the lives of those who heard them. One woman whose loved one's life was taken by another family member was not able to forgive, even after he spent time in prison. But as she heard the poem, the Lord gave her the strength to forgive him. She even went further and embraced her brother as a new member of the family. Then she did even more, blessing him with enough provisions to get him started again. Her brother was so overwhelmed with great joy that he gave his life to Jesus. Praise God!

My desire is that these poems will transform people's lives, and they will realize that God is intimately involved in the lives that are surrendered to him.

These words address myriad issues I went through, including holding an unforgiving spirit, fear, barrenness, lack of faith, anxiousness, fatherlessness, prayerlessness, and failure. Some of us are faced with these same problems, and we just want to hear one word from the Lord to remind us that He is always with us in our struggles, gives grace for every storm, and redirects us to the right path.

The writing of these poems was not spontaneous. Sometimes when I tried to write a line, nothing happened; no words would flow. At other times, I might have been riding the train, doing household chores, and or worshipping God, and the words just dropped into my spirit. I learned to recognize this voice, the voice of the Lord. The sweetest, most generous, and most tender voice of God ushered into my spirit. I would immediately hear at least the skeleton of the poem and then began to quickly write what I heard on whatever paper was readily available. This did not happen as often as I wanted it to, so it took me about eighteen months to write this book. The poems may be short, but they are so precious to me for they have given me the answers I sought from God during my period of darkness. Even now, sometimes when I am having a difficult time, I read these poems for comfort.

However, there is no substitute for the scriptures; we need to read God's Word daily. We will never be able to survive the evil enchantments of this world without having a daily dose of the Bible. It is so imperative to dig deep into what the Word says, meditate on it as we go to sleep, and speak it often. When I learned that the Word of God is the key to survival, I compelled my spirit to seek hard after this precious gem for which there is absolutely no substitute.

God has a unique calling for everyone. It may not be to document what He says on a regular basis, but there is a purpose for every life. We are not here by accident. We were carefully planned and laid out by God before the foundations of the earth. He even knew us before we were born, as we lay in our mothers' wombs.

Wherever you are in your in spiritual life with the Lord, these poems can propel you to that safe place of trusting God for all our provisions. For the person who has the deep desire of going deeper and facing daily struggles of addictions, setbacks, or failures, let the unique message of these poems permeate your inner spirit as it refocuses your mind on things that are really important and of eternal value.

"And thy ears shall hear a word behind thee, saying, this is the way walk in it when he turn to the right hand and when he turn to the left." (Isaiah 30:21)

PROPHETIC POEM 1

What if I Tell you That?

What if I tell you that I will turn your barrenness into
 fruitfulness?
What if I tell you that weeping may endure for a night, but
 joy comes in the morning? I will turn your mourning into
 dancing.
What if I tell you that I will restore the years that the locusts
 have eaten?
What if I tell you I will do it again, and that your best days are
 before you and not behind?
What if I tell you the stone that the builders refuse will become
 the head cornerstone?
What if I tell you that you are the righteousness of God through
 Jesus Christ?
I love you with an everlasting love, and with love have I
 drawn you.
The joy of the Lord is your strength.
I will anoint you with the oil of gladness.
I created you for My purpose only!
All who were against you shall become nothing.
I will never leave you; neither will I forsake you.
You are the apple of My eyes.
The same power that raises Christ from the dead lives in you.
You are a vineyard of red wine.

With a long life will I satisfy you?
You are more than a conqueror through Jesus Christ.
I forgive all your iniquities and heal all your diseases.
I will redeem your life from destruction.
I will satisfy thy mouth with good things so that thy youth is
    renewed like the eagles.

My Response to Prophetic Poem 1

One day I pondered all my mishaps in life, especially deferred dreams and not having sufficiency in all things. Or so I thought at the moment. The Lord burst into my thoughts in a forceful way and said these words to me, which I wrote in "Prophetic Poem 1." I was amazed that as the Lord kept showering me with these words from the scriptures, all my wonderings became of less importance, and God's words became the anchor during my storms. It is so important that we read the scriptures and let its miraculous power go into our minds, clean out all the impurities, refresh, and position us to reap the promises God destined for our lives. You will be amazed to see the results of this purification process deep within your inner spirit. I can assure you, you will have the mind of God, seeing things from His perspective rather than how the world expects you to analyze the day's happenings. Your eyes will be so focused on things of God as the old self-nature dies.

There is a great sense of peace that all is well even amid the storm. You can find suitable scriptures and use them to boldly speak to any adverse circumstances you may face. If you are being tormented by a spirit of fear, decree that the righteous are as bold as lions, and the wicked flee when no one pursues. If you struggle with thought of an untimely death in any form, you may find scriptures such as Psalm 91:16, "with long life will I satisfy you," helpful.

Let the remedy you seek be found in God's powerful Word. Read it daily, and speak His words over yourself. If you are a newborn Christian, begin by reading a small portion daily, and ask the Lord exactly what He wants you to get from that portion of scriptures. I usually decree them for my students and say they can do all things through Christ. I have seen them move from a place of failure to having success in many areas of their academic studies. You will find comfort in Hebrews 4:12: "the word of God is quick and powerful and sharper than any two edged sword," and in Psalm 119:130, "the entrance of thy words give light."

PROPHETIC POEM 2

The Loving Father God, Speaking to His Child

My love, all I have is yours, and you are Mine.

You are rich beyond measure, and your cup overflows over continually.

While the stars shine most brightly when it is dark, so I stay closest to you in your deepest moments of despair.

Seek after Me with all your heart, and you will find Me.

Even if I hide for a moment, I will come so that you may rest your weary head on My shoulder.

My child, what do you seek today?

Is it love, peace, fulfillment, safety, friendship, healing, freedom, joy?

Speak it, and I will give it according to My riches in glory.

My Response to Prophetic Poem 2

Have you ever felt hopeless, even when you hear the promises of God over and over? God spoke these words to me so gently, as if I was a little child, sitting on His lap, being cuddled with lots of fatherly love. I felt that deep inner peace as I quieted my spirit and listened to His comforting words. I believe these loving words of the Father entered my spirit realm as a seed settling into the ground, waiting for germination, without the soil knowing what was to burst forth in a short time.

Always spend time with the Lord, and wait quietly for Him. Turn off the day's events, along with the technological gadgets. Don't rush Him with your busy schedule. God does not operate in the microwave world of instant gratification. The seed takes time to germinate in the ground. God wants to do a work in us for His purpose, and I think the only thing we need to do for God is to give Him time. Spend time with Him, not just praying or worshipping, but also to be involved in direct conversation. I usually ask Him lots of questions and tell Him all my concerns. Of course, I know God already knows all thoughts, but I developed the habit of talking to Him just like I was standing beside and relating to a physical person. If God is really my Father, why do I have to wait for a grand invitation to meet with Him? It is all about relationship!

PROPHETIC POEM 3

When You Come into My Presence Today, Remember To ...

Wear the garment of praise for God inhabits your praises.
Wear the robe of righteousness; live a life of holiness.
Wear the helmet of salvation; keep your mind protected from
   whatever thoughts the enemy may inflict on you.
Wear the breastplate of righteousness; guard your heart for out
   of it all the issues of life flows.
Wear the belt of truth; keep your intentions and motives pure
   and truthful for our relationship to be intact.
Wear the perfume of myrrh and spices so that true worship can
   spontaneously take place at all times.
The King's daughter is all glorious, all beautiful, and all
   delightful to behold.
The King's daughter is all glorious.
Let Me dress you today!

My Response to Prophetic Poem 3

God wants us to be clothed in His righteousness, not our own. As we begin to acknowledge Him as Lord and Savior over our lives, read His Word, and pray, we are being robed in garments of His righteousness. This is not something we do but mainly what God's nature is. We become righteous when we live a life holy and acceptable to Him.

PROPHETIC POEM 4

Someone Needs You Today

Someone needs you today!
To speak peace during a time of chaos for them.
To shine your light so others can see the way.
To open the door so they may enter.
To declare God's words over those who are cast down.
To be the only Jesus they will ever see.
So prepare your spirit in a way that will touch the hearts of all
   those who will purposely come in contact with you.
You are entrusted with lives in which you are responsible for their
   eternal purposes.
Will you lead them to the peace that they have been searching for?
Will you hold their hands even when yours are hurting?
Will you allow them to know Jesus and the power of My
   resurrection?
Someone needs you today.
To whom much is given, much is required.
You are the one who has been sent to them.
Someone needs you today!

My Response to Prophetic Poem 4

The Lord wants us to realize that we are not here by accident but are purposely placed in this world for such a time as this. Think about the fact that there is this urgency for you to be used by God. Whatever we do, we must work while it is still day as Jesus said. The workers are needed in the fields, and as the Savior asks, "who will go for Him?" Isaiah 6v.8 (emphasis added)

After writing this poem, I thought of how many difficult tasks the Lord has asked of me over the years. Some I have willingly done, while others I have not even attempted because of fear. Today I ask the Lord to forgive me and promise never to let Him down again. I remember a loved one who was gravely ill. I knelt at my bedside, praying for her healing. I saw a vision of two angels over her in the hospital and immediately knew she was healed. The doctor who scheduled her for surgery had her discharged since she was well.

I had this same experience the same the following year. I was praying for another gravely ill loved one and had an amazingly awesome sight of Jesus's pierced side. This was so real. As I prayed for her, who was given a negative doctor's report, all I could see in my dreams was death for her. So I knelt by my bedside, praying over her life. As I did so, over and over the answer came. I saw Jesus's pierced side and pleaded with the blood of Jesus on behalf of my sister. I was not alarmed and felt a sense of peace and that the task was accomplished. At that moment, I knew that He wanted me to know she would live. I called and prayed with her, and immediately, she praised God for the miracle.

I did not see His face, only His pierced side. The gaping wound was still there, not closed as we would imagine. It was the size of a grapefruit and maroon red in color. The edges of the wound seemed to be curve slightly forward, like a squeezed grapefruit. While the

11

wound was still open, it was not messy. He was not black or white in color, as many people might think. He was bronze, or maroon reddish, in color. Up to today, I kept a bottle I had that matches the color and size of the gaping in His side.

The memory of the gaping in Jesus's side remains vivid to this day. This is reality; Jesus died and shed His precious blood for us all. Jesus did not show me His pierced side because I was spiritually important; I don't claim to be that. Instead, He showed me this to say that only He has the power to heal.

PROPHETIC POEM 5

I Want You to Forgive

Because it will cause all your prayers to be answered,
Because you will be able to bind and loose in my name,
Because you will have My continual peace residing in you,
Because your joy will be full,
Because you will hear My voice more clearly,
Because you will discern the good from the evil,
Because your heart will be pure and true,
Because you will escape the plots of the enemy,
Because your mind will be set on Me,
Because your mind will be set on things above and not beneath,
Because the days of your life will be prolonged,
Because love will flow out naturally, like a fountain of cool crisp
    clear water,
Because you will heap coals of fire on your enemies' heads,
Because the Father wants to enjoy His child without blemish or
    spots,
Because I have forgiven you first,
Because there is nothing more powerful than a forgiving heart.

If you have brought your gift to Me, God, first forgive all those
    who have maliciously hurt you before you offer it.
Begin the forgiveness process today so that the inner healing can
    take place deep within.
This is not a choice; this is the only way out. Many have lost
    the most precious thing—their souls—because they refuse to
    trust Me to keep it safe.

Ananias was worried about forgiving Paul for all the evil he inflicted on the early Christians, but Paul could not be used until Ananias had truly forgiven (accepted) him and prayed for him. Can you see how many lives can be set free if you could truly forgive? Remember, if you want to be forgiven, you must first forgive.

My Response to Prophetic Poem 5

When the Lord gave me these words, I did not know they were supposed to be for a close family member who was struggling with these issues. Immediately after she heard these words of forgiving others, she was ready to forgive the person who caused her much pain. To forgive those who have viciously hurt us is difficult, but when we truly have the spirit of love, we will forgive others.

Sometimes we refuse to forgive someone for a simple error when we have also caused great hurt to others and need forgiveness, too. I struggle with this issue, and the words of this poem made me realize that not forgiving those who have hurt us would not put us in right standing with God. We would miss out on the blessings that God has for our lives, so forgiving others benefits us in a great way. We must ask the Lord to give us grace to forgive others, and God will give us grace to forgive all others and even ourselves.

Sometimes you may not feel able to forgive others. But just be honest with God, the Father. Come to Him humbly, and let Him know that you are not able to forgive, so you are giving the issues to Him. When we have truly forgiven someone, the hurt is not present anymore. A peace fills your heart and causes you to love the person. I strongly believe true forgiveness gives birth to freedom in Jesus.

PROPHETIC POEM 6

What Do You Want to Keep Today?

What do you want to keep today?
Is it your talents?
Is it your friends?
Is it your spouse?
Is it your loved ones?
Is it your dreams?
Is it your riches?
Is it your job?
Is it your life?
Is it your soul?
Then if you do, you may not really have it; only what is given
to Me, God, will be of value to you.

My Response to Prophetic Poem 6

The only thing that is safe is what is truly first given up to the Lord. Why? Because God doesn't want any of the gifts He has given us to defile our love for Him. We see this with Abraham. After he waited for many years to have a child, he had to obey God and present his precious Isaac as a sacrifice. The famous theologian A. W. Tozer helped me to understand the pain and agony Abraham had to endure in the giving up of his long-awaited son. In his book *The Pursuit of God*, Tozer shares that God never intended to actually kill Isaac but just remove him from that special place in Abraham's heart, so God could reign unchallenged.

Some of us will willingly heed the loving request of our Lord to give Him first place, while others will unfortunately neglect this plea and face serious consequences. We must learn to trust the Lord with our treasures, whether they are our loved ones, jobs, or wealth. Only He can keep them safe. Jesus said that where your treasures are, there will be your heart. One of my greatest fears is to hold on to things because I know I will surely lose it. I vividly remember when I moved into my new home. For the first month, I was so overjoyed that each morning I wanted to first look at my garden to see the beautiful roses and the manicured lawn. But I had to force myself to first read the Word of God, pray, and praise before leaving my bedroom. After a while, I lost all that excitement for houses and beautifully manicured lawns. God became my greatest awe and excitement. I thank God that I was able to put Him in first place.

All I am saying is let God be first, and trust Him with all your treasures. God works uniquely with each of His children, so we must be sensitive to His voice. I am not talking of legalism, where you follow a set of rules to get to God. God is interested in having a relationship with His children and has His unique ways to speak to your heart, allow you to know where you are going wrong, and to pull you back. We must not make one broad generalization to judge every situation in our lives. But we have to use the Holy Spirit's wisdom to guide our actions. I cannot tell you that going to the movies, wearing tattoos, or practicing yoga is wrong or right. I can tell you with surety that whatever we do must be done to the glory of God. What I am saying here is that God did not relate to me under legalism but through a loving relationship.

PROPHETIC POEM 7

If You Ever Feel Afraid ...

Know that fear is only a feeling, and we walk by faith and not
by sight.
So trust in God, and all fears will go for perfect love casts out fear.
Know that even in the darkness you have Me, God. Therefore, I
say, fear though not; I will be with you.
Know that there is more with you than with the enemy.
Know that even when the fear of failure strikes you, just knowing
Me as Lord is the greatest success one could ever achieve.
You will be like the tree planted by the rivers of water, and
whatsoever you do will prosper.
Know when the fear of sickness whispers in your ear and says it's
over, your body is already my temple. So fear will find no safe
space to dwell. I send My Word and heal all your diseases.
Know that when the fear of humans commands you to bow at
someone's feet, I say the righteous are as bold as a lion, but
the wicked flee when no one pursues.
Know that when the fear of death tries to crumble your world
to pieces, I say you will live and not die to declare the works
of the Lord.
Know that when the fears of this world seek to inflict worries and
torments upon you, My child, just give them up to Me for
I say, cast all your cares upon Me, God, for I care for you.
When you do, give it a date. Whenever these spirits try to
return, remember the date you handed them over and say,
"God, have that fear," each time it tries to reenter.
Surrender all your fears, big or small, to Me, God.

Know that fear, big or small, is the enemy's only weapon, and he
has not been able to come up with a new one since creation.
It just manifests in millions of forms and will have power if we
open the door for it to enter.
We only need to believe fear, and the door is immediately swung
wide open again to all its torments.
But my greatest weapon is faith, and that is all the answer you
will need.
Keep a watchful heart as our hearts have eyes to discern.
Keep your mind set on God, and watch the spirit of fear become
too fearful to attack.
Remember Job's greatest fears came upon him.
Watch out for the things you fear, and have them surrender to
Me, God.
Remember, perfect love casts out all fear!

My Response to Prophetic Poem 7

The spirit of fear has attacked me constantly, usually wielded debilitating blows. At times, my world crumbles in a split second when these horrible thoughts come into my mind. I was also afraid of being in the dark and going to funerals. I even feared spirits of loved ones who passed way would return as ghosts and torment me. Some years ago, a loved one passed away tragically. I received the dreaded news at work. The grief was unbearable, and so was the fear. I was devastated and fearful, so I came home and watched a particular program on Christian TV. The presenter, a famous man of God, was praying. Then he stopped and said, "Someone has a spirit of fear. They are afraid of the dark, they are of the night ... and this fear is leaving them right now in Jesus's name." I know this was for me. Since that day, I have not been afraid of the dark or the night.

However, fear later attacked me in many other forms. I had endless fears because I was always surrounded by words of fear. Then one day, God spoke these words of "Prophetic Poem 7" to reassure me that a spirit of fear will not have dominion over me. I must press into faith and know that God has not given me this spirit of fear. I have seen times when fear will leave and return in another form, but during this time, I have to trust God to take care of my fears. One of my favorite scriptures is Isaiah 41:10: "Fear thou not for I am with thee." I believe this scripture was designed with me in mind because that was what broke the power of this tormenting spirit on me.

I vividly remember my fear of traveling on airplanes. As soon as I boarded the plane, the deceptive voice of the enemy entered my mind. I realized I had to pull the plug on these thoughts. One day as I boarded an airplane, fear wrapped its tentacles around my mind as usual. As I sat belted in my seat, it was announced over the flight intercom that the plane had some computer issues and would be delayed. I knew I had to make the decision to put a stop to this fear immediately. It was my time to either act on the Word of God or just allow my fears to hold me captive. I took out my Bible fearfully but in defiance of this spirit of fear. And in a loud and boisterous voice, I read some chapters in the book of Isaiah for about half an hour. The passenger beside me sat with his eyes closed. Then he opened his eyes, smiled and asked, "Is that the book of Isaiah you are reading from?" I believe he knew I was fearful. Since that day, I have not been afraid of airplanes. A miracle took place that day, and I thank God for helping me to overcome this fear of flying.

I believe the person who places trust in God is continuously protected from all harm, whether in the sky, land, or sea. God has so many plans for us, and we need to break free from this spirit of fear so we can accomplish much.

Most times these fears are difficult to discern. Elijah, a very powerful man of God, was a great prophet, but he was taken over by the same spirit of fear. One of the most effective weapons against this spirit of fear is to apply faith in all areas of life. If you are battling this spirit, surround yourself with a faith-filled atmosphere. We don't talk fear, but we talk faith. We don't sow seeds that will produce fear. Negative and useless conversations produce fear. What are your conversations like? Are they always about something negative? We live in a world where this is difficult because news reports are usually fearful. But we can be like Daniel and propose in our hearts to refuse the things that defile us. Stop listening to the news does not remove fear for it will just find another door to enter through. All our actions have to be surrendered to the Lord. That is what Paul means when he said to present our bodies as living sacrifices so that God can do the work for us. Also we have to resist, and it will flee and offer no ways to entertain that spirit.

PROPHETIC POEM 8

I Will Use Barrenness To ...

I will use barrenness to sculpture and shape you into your place
of purpose and destiny.

I will use barrenness to cause fruitfulness to take place, so you
can declare that you are a vineyard of red wine.

I will use barrenness to cause you to sow seeds into the fields of
impossibility because with Me, God, nothing is impossible.

I will use barrenness to cause you to reap tears of joy and gain
new strength to overcome.

I will use barrenness to cause you to multiply in every form and
realm.

Remember, barrenness is the ladder that you climb to reach your
place of right standing with Me.

Everyone I have used possessed some form of barrenness. It is
that dark, dull, and uneasy period in one's life that causes
My plan to come to fruition.

It is that period of pain of suffering when you think that I have
forsaken you, but I am molding and forming you during this
time. The pain will feel unbearable, but the glory that will
come from this is immeasurable.

Before I use anyone, I cause barrenness to take place in their lives
so that they will see that without Me, they can do nothing.
Look at Sarah, Hannah, and Elisabeth. Examine the mighty
fruits that I caused them to produce, and so I will cause an
even mightier fruit to be grown in My people at this time.

Barrenness in the physical is not an issue, but it is being barren
spiritually when I am expecting to you to bear fruit. After

the tree has been pruned many times it remains barren, the tree becomes purposeless.

The tree must serve its purpose of bearing fruit, laden not with beautiful leaves but with fruit so others can partake.

So what prevents you from bearing fruit today?

What keeps you from entering daily into My presence so you can bear fruit? I do not require a gift but a fruit. Pass the places that have been holding you back, and enter freely. Learn to desire the things that I desire. Learn to be free from the weight that holds you down. Open your heart to My spirit, and let Me fine-tune you in to My words. All things work together for good to those who love God and all called toward His purpose.

> "Sing thou barren that bears not, break forth and cry thou that travails not for the desolate hath many more children than she which hath an husband." (Isaiah 54V.1

My Response to Prophetic Poem 8

My deepest heart cry has always been to overcome physical barrenness. God has continuously reassured me that barrenness is the tool He is using to use to shape me. This will result in me bearing fruit. My form of physical barrenness was infertility. Any woman who has gone through this will tell you there is no greater pain. You get to see all your friends' children and grandchildren, but you never get to see your offspring. You will go to bed crying and wake up crying. You put a smile on your face, hoping that no one sees the pain. You hide this pain so securely from even your closest loved ones. They will never know that you are hurting so deeply.

This period of barrenness has not been a failure for me for it is through that pain I get to talk to God and want to share my heart with Him more and more daily. During this desperate time, God has done a marvelous heart transformation inside me. The transformation has been incredible; from a heart of stone in me, He has placed a heart of flesh. I have been given a new perspective on how I see things. Everything must be perceived how God wants me to perceive them. I do not just merely exist and occupy space on earth. I was born for a purpose, and no one else will be able to serve that specific purpose. I get to spend time in conversation with the Lord and realize how much He has blessed me spiritually and other ways.

If you are waiting for God to do something for you—whether in your health, marriage, children, or job—wait patiently for Him. He will surely come to heal the situation one way or another. Some of us lack so many things, but we must remember the one thing we truly need is to have peace with God. To do His will. What will happen to us when we take our last breaths if we don't have peace with God? Where will we go? This is scary! I thank God every day for the promise of eternal life through His precious Son, Jesus. Count every other accomplishment as nothing until you make peace with God. Remember, the Lord has specific tools He uses to shape us, and we must be sensitive and open to what He is doing in our lives. However, I am still waiting for God to bless me with children again. Although God is more interested in character building than a comfortable lifestyle.

PROPHETIC POEM 9

I Am Pleased with You Today Because ...

You have been like Mary, sitting at My feet to hear what I have to say. Even when there is so much to be done, you have set aside time for Me. You have not allowed busyness to rob My fellowship with you. Like I said to Mary, you have chosen the better part.

You have been like Job, going through the greatest storm, losing so much of yourself. And still you say that your latter shall be greater. Remember, you will always receive double for your trouble because you have placed your trust in God.

You have been like Moses, just wanting to know Me and My ways, even when only a few desire this path of going deeper.

You have been like Daniel, purposed in your heart not to be contaminated by the things of this world. Yet you have seen the dainties of this world, which I hate, and you choose to partake of My table of sanctification and holiness.

You have been like Noah and spent all your life in building the ark for the day of calamity, knowing that the only safe place for you will be with Me.

You have been like Nehemiah, engulfed by a troubling sensation that the walls need to be to be rebuilt again for you and your generation.

You have been like Paul, knowing he was shipwrecked, beaten, arrested, and bitten by snakes; yet he said none of these things moved him as Paul said "If I live, I live for God, and if I die, I die for God."

You have been like Isaiah, allowing the things you care about to die, so you can see the Lord high and lifted up, far above you and above your circumstances, so worship can have the center place in your heart.

You have been like Abraham, knowing that to truly please God is to place your most treasured things on the sacrificial altar, even when it rips your heart apart. But this is the only way to give up all you hold dear, so they can be released back to you.

My Response to Prophetic Poem 9

I hear the Lord echo these words of accomplishment in my spirit, and I didn't think I was able to measure up to these words because I falter daily in my spiritual life. But, you see, the Lord speaks prophetically by speaking things into being. He called this world into existence by saying, "Let there be light, and there was light." Genesis 1v.3. He did not wonder if light would ever come; He called it forth into existence, and that is the pattern He lay out for us to emulate. The scriptures tell us to call those things that are not as if they were (Romans 4:17).

Many years ago, I was driving from work and having a conversation with God. I told Him that I was so fearful and not able to really accomplish much for Him. God gave me a surprising answer: "I don't see you as fearful but very strong. You must see yourself like how I see you." We must see ourselves as God sees us; bold as a lion and able to all things through Christ, who strengthens us. This was the reassurance I needed to keep pressing on.

PROPHETIC POEM 10

Come unto Me

I will give you rest. Take My yoke for My burden is easy, and
My yoke is light.
Why do you worry and fear about the issues of life?
Are the circumstances bigger than Me?
Am I not a God at hand and not far off?
Is there any situation too big for Me?
Why do you think that My hand is not enough to save you? I
told you that My peace will go with you wherever you go.
Even if you are in the deepest pit of despair, there I will be
with you.
My plans for you are plans of peace to prosper you.
So come unto Me, and rest sweetly in My arms.
There you will find peace for your mind.
My love for you is everlasting, and so is My Word over you.

There is a safe place from the storm, a place where the fiercest of
lions have not trodden.
So come unto Me, and surrender it all.

My Response to Prophetic Poem 10

If you ever doubt that God will come to your rescue immediately, read this poem over and over. Allow it to saturate your spirit realm. Sometimes God doesn't remove storms because they are there to test us. But He assured us that He is in the midst of the storm. How else will we be able to soar like eagles? The scripture speaks about the eagle that prepares and teaches her young chicks the life skills needed for their survival by constantly making them so uncomfortable in the nest: "As the eagle stirred up her nest, fluttered over her young, spread aboard her wings, take them, bear them on her wings." (Deuteronomy 32:11).

The Lord God does the same with His children by ripping us out of our comfort zones. The uncomfortable circumstances we face mature our faith. We must bear fruit if we are saved. And even when we bear fruit, we are pruned to bear more and more fruit, as described in John 15:2. The process of cutting of branches from the overcrowded tree in order to bear more fruit is not pleasant. However, the goal is not to destroy the tree but to have it produce.

PROPHETIC POEM 11

Believing Is Receiving

Whatever you believe you will receive for believing is receiving!

Whatever a man thinks so is he; think peace, think joy, think
only what you want to enter your spirit realm for believing
is receiving.

If you believe your prayers are answered, you will receive as you
believe.

Think on whatever things are true, honest, and just.

The moment you believe you will receive. What you believe you
will receive.

Therefore, believe only the good report, which is of God.

Say aloud that you will only believe the report of God, who says
all is well through His Word.

My Response to Prophetic Poem 11

"Therefore I say unto you whatever he desires believe that he received them and he shall have them." (Mark 11:24)

PROPHETIC POEM 12

The Hiding Place

Lord God, You are my hiding place.

Your arms covered me in every storm.

I will be with you when you pass through the waters.

I will be with you through the rivers, and they shall not overflow you.

I will be with you when you walk through fires, so you will not be burned.

I will go before you and make every crooked place straight.

I will break in pieces the gates of brass and cut asunder the bars of iron.

No one shall be able to withstand My anointed presence in you today.

For I say your best years are yet to come, and you shall finish strongly and triumphantly.

Hear ye My words today, and let them resonate in your spirit realm for the stones that the builders refused have now become the head cornerstone.

As it was in the beginning, so it will be now as I am the Lord and I change not.

My anointed presence will go with you.

I have prepared for you a place of safety, though you feel like you have been tossed and blown by the fiercest wind; that's part of the plan to keep you resurrected.

At times, you feel like you have been roasted on an open flame, but that is just to prevent you from growing cold, so you can keep hot and My presence can dwell in you.

At times, you remain silent for many will not understand your story; as Mary had to ponder many things within her heart, so will you.

My Response to Prophetic Poem 12

There is a hiding place in God. The scriptures speak about this place in Job 28:7–8: "There is a path which no fowl knows and which the vultures eyes hath not seen: the lions whelps have not trodden nor the fierce lion passed by it." This is the haven you have when you are dependent on God's protection. God has a protection plan for us, and that is why we must trust Him and by faith know we are safe. We will go through fires, struggles, tests, setbacks, and all other negative occurrences, but we will come out without even the smell of fire on us. This protection goes for all areas of business or personal life.

PROPHETIC POEM 13

Today Is the Best Day of Your Life

Today, when you awoke and saw the sun shining, you realized that you have the chance of bringing the light to all those in the darkness who may hear your voice.

Today you have the chance to accept My forgiveness and let Me wipe the slate clean, like it never happened.

Today you have the chance to make it right with all those around you who have hurt you and caused you great pain.

Today you can have the chance to govern your words and thoughts, so your words will pour out like liquid gold, pure and undiluted.

Today you have the chance to decide how you will spend the rest of your life; make decisions wisely to affect your eternal destination.

So what will you do with today?

For today is the day you really have.

Whose lives will be changed today by your words of peace?

Whose broken hearts will be mended today as they see that you care?

What will happen to those who are stricken in grief and not able to understand why their loved ones are not around?

Will you be able to hold them up and let them know that I will strengthen them for I give power to the faint and those who have no might because I am the strength of their lives?

What about those who are oppressed, depressed, and tormented by the enemy?

Will they be able to hear the good news that Jesus has come to
set the captives free?
And remember the ones who are about to enter eternity in the
next minute.
Will you let them know that Jesus saves?
That Jesus died for them and wants to redeem them from a life
of destruction?
Spend today wisely.
It is a gift to you.
Today is the day you really have!

My Response to Prophetic Poem 13

As the Lord spoke these words to me, I had no idea why He was so intensely pressing these strong words into my inner spirit at the time. Then a few days later, I heard that someone I knew was gravely ill, and the Lord wanted me to pray for her salvation. As I was about to have dinner, I sensed a great burden in my spirit, like I always do whenever someone is dying without Christ. So I left my dinner and began to cry and pray until I felt peace. I knew that she was safe now one way or the other.

I want to make every day count for Jesus. We must see every day as a day of opportunity to bring the lost to Christ, to speak peace into chaos, and to bring the light of Jesus into a dark world. No matter how people resent us, they are waiting for us to bring light to them. The good news is that Jesus saves, heals, and delivers. We are His hands and feet, and He is not using angels to do this job. He sent Peter to Cornelius's house. Peter had so many prejudices that God had to give him a dream showing He had great plans for Cornelius.

Where would I be today if God had not shown me His grace and mercy? Every minute is extremely important, and if is not for you, it is for someone else who needs to hear the good news. I was watching a famous televangelist make one of his regular altar calls. Those who are familiar with this evangelist will realize that his one and only business is to call sinners to Christ. He shared a story of an encounter he had while a visiting church. After he called for people to come forward to be saved; there were two men remaining who needed to be saved. After waiting awhile, both came up, said prayed the sinners' prayer, and accepted Jesus. Later, after the evangelist returned to his home church, the pastor for the church he visited told him those men died the same night. They did not know each other when they were alive, but now they both went to heaven. One was older and died in his sleep, while the other died during a drive-by shooting.

This horrific scenario woke me spiritually to realize that we have a serious job to do. There are times when I know I have shirked my responsibilities and the most important things of God by not telling others about Jesus as the Holy Spirit led me because of fears or because I just didn't care. I have repented of this, and today I desire to be on fire for the Lord as every true believer is a soul winner for Christ.

PROPHETIC POEM 14

May the Eyes of Your Understanding Be Enlightened

Be enlightened to know Me, God.
Be enlightened to know what My plans are for you.
Be enlightened to know the greatness of My power.
Be enlightened to understand your calling and purpose, so you
    can fulfill your destiny.
May the eyes of your understanding be enlightened today!

Let Me enlighten your path today for the path of the righteous
    grows brighter and brighter.
If you find that you are not able to see clearly, allow Me to
Shine My light onto your path.
Spend time with Me, God, in meditation and prayer, and watch
    how those things that appeared to have been misunderstood
    now become perceivable.
Will you let Me enlighten the eyes of your understanding today?

My Response to Prophetic Poem 14

The Lord gave me these words for someone I came in contact with who is saved and yet struggles with the idea that God is able to use Christian books as a tool to spread His Word. She told me that God does not need us to read books by Christian writers since He has already placed everything in His Word. But I know that God uses Christian authors to spread His Word in their books. Paul read books, too. I have read a number of books from various Christian authors, and I know that the spirit of God speaks through them.

> "That the God of our Lord Jesus Christ, the Father of glory may give unto you the spirit of wisdom and revelation in the knowledge of Him." (Ephesians 1:17)

I pray for the spirit of wisdom and revelation to be upon my life always.

PROPHETIC POEM 15

Your Faith

Your faith is all I need to deliver you today.
Will I be able to find faith when I come to deliver you?
If your faith is weak, read My Word to strengthen your weak
faith.
If your faith needs to be nourished, speak My Word aloud in
every situation.
If your faith needs to be matured, act on My Word, so the
mountains around you can be removed.
Will I be able to find faith when I come to deliver you today?
Faith is not the absence of storms; in fact, without storms, you
may never have great faith.
With faith, we don't fear the effects of the fire, even when we are
standing in its flames.
We know there is a power greater than what we see or feel.
We know that even if the floods have lifted their voices, your God
on high is mightier than the noise of many waters.
See the floods as powerless over you and your God as all powerful
in you.
Without the storms, you may never get the chance to develop,
grow, and mature in Me.
Remember, the greater the storm, so will your faith be; the
intensity of your storm determines the level of your faith.
While you may not welcome the storm, you will see it was
necessary for your growth and maturity.
Let me ask you again, will I be able to find faith when I come to
deliver you today?
Miracles can only be done in the presence of faith.

My Response to Prophetic Poem 15

When the Lord spoke these words to me, I had no idea that this was scriptural, coming from Luke 18:8 at the time. A few months later, I heard the verse for the first time, and then I made the connection. God never speaks outside of His Word, and that is why we have to read the Bible and meditate to understand the mind of God.

I face a daily spiritual battle with constant attacks by the enemy. A few minutes before I wrote these words, I was having a difficult morning at work. I wanted to run and hide somewhere—maybe in a cave—just to have peace. But the Lord spoke to me in a very serious, fatherly tone, and I wrote "Prophetic Poem 15." He wanted me to have strong faith by using the scripture to counter every attack. The sole purposes of these attacks, as painful as they were, was to build my faith. I understand now, even more clearly, that we must see our God as more powerful than all our circumstances. God intends to build us, not to destroy us, and He can only work with our faith.

I keep remembering that when the apostle Paul was shipwrecked, he reminded those around him that was not the end for God had told him he was going to deliver a message to Caesar. We must remember the plans that God has for us and, by faith, use the scriptures that go with these promises. Our circumstances may be different and seem unbearable at times, but the remedy is always the same. Faith in God will conquer all things. Jesus can do no mighty work where faith is absent.

PROPHETIC POEM 16

Be Still

If I can get you to be still, I can get you whole, healed, and
delivered.
If I can get you to be still, you will receive the
answers that you have been seeking as I will reveal them to you
in the stillness of your mind.

If I can get you to be still, I can have you forget the past and set
your mind on the task before you.
If I can get you to be still, you will know when to wait on Me for
provisions for your journey ahead.
Let stillness allow you to flourish and eat the good of the land.
Decide that you will not be anxious, but you will trust Me to
give you the desires of your heart.

Why is being still that important for our relationship? Because
that is the time when your spirit listens to My voice.
That's the time when your spirit hears Me clearly and comes in
full agreement with Me.
Will you be still today?
Will you put aside the cares of this life and listen to Me for a
moment?
That may be the moment you will get the directions you have
been seeking for your journey ahead. Even runners have to
be stilled those few moments before they run their races. So
can you imagine how stillness is important before you set off
on your course?

Make a decision today that for the rest of your life, you will choose stillness over worry.

Stillness is obedience.

Stillness is humility.

Stillness is power over your mind.

So begin to take small steps of stillness until you are able to take bigger steps.

Oh, the benefits of stillness are rewarding.

A stilled spirit is one that is living a life filled with purpose and destiny and able to perceive the future with great faith.

The next time you attempt to pray, still your spirit before you utter the words.

Let Me pray within you as before you ask, I know the desires of your heart.

That means three powerful words: stop, wait, and listen.

They who wait upon the Lord shall renew their strength.

My soul waits upon the Lord.

My Response to Prophetic Poem 16

Have you ever been so busy just thinking your situation through and hoping to find an answer? That what was happening with me when the Lord interpreted my thoughts and said just two powerful words: "Be still." I find that being still means just what it says. Let God do the thinking because He has all the answers. We surrender that issue to Him, and stop thinking about it. The enemy wants us to go crazy, thinking of all the possible solutions, but God wants our spirits to be quiet, so He can fill us with whatever answers we seek. Some of us are bombarded by the second with all manner of thoughts, such as fear, pornography, and suicidal ideation. But we must be still and submit. The more our thoughts run wild, the more power over us we give the enemy. Practice the habit of stillness.

King David says, "Surely I have behaved and quieted myself as a child that is weaned of his mother; my soul is even as a weaned child" (Psalm 131:2). The weaned child behaves more responsibly and is not worried about trying to get the mother's milk he or she desires all time of the day or night when younger. The weaned child is able to wait for the normal set mealtime.

Our Father God expects us to grow in maturity by developing patience and knowing that all is well in Jesus's name. Command your mind and spirit to be still.

PROPHETIC POEM 17

Yes, I Will Show You Favor

Favor begins with obedience when you listen to My commands and follow them.
It's more than receiving the ordinary; it is the extraordinary.
Some people receive the ordinary, while some receive the extraordinary.

Joseph did not receive the ordinary; instead, he received the extraordinary.
Joseph received the most beautiful of all the twelve coats, and that is what being obedient will do for you, too.
All the coats were not of equal worth or value.
These were favors, not coats, and signs that Joseph was being used by God then and in the future.
Jesus had twelve disciples, and only one was called His beloved. Wow!

Favor is the reward for being obedient.
Favor is I being well pleased and overjoyed with you.
If you are willing and obedient, you will eat the good of the land!
Have you been humble in all you do? Then expect a giant burst of favor to overflow on you today.
Have you shown kindness to the most unlikely persons? Then expect kindness to spring up like wildflowers in your path today.
Have you been that cheerful giver in both your words and deeds? Then you will reap bundles of provisions, and your storehouse will never be empty.

Have you prayed for those who are set against you today? If so, expect favor to surround you as a shield.

Have you been that person to visit the sick and those in prison? Then you may never find yourself in that situation and need to be visited.

It's all wrapped up in your obedience.

So expect favor even more today.

What areas do you need to see My favor in today?

Begin to receive not just the normal but more and more!

With My favor, you will never receive a negative report; for you, My report says all is well, even in the midst of the storm.

With My favor, you will never be in need for you know that the Lord is your shepherd; and you will never have a want for anything. The Good Shepherd takes care of His fold continuously.

With My favor, you will never need to worry for your answers are already there, even when the natural eyes don't see them.

As Mary and the others were about to anoint Jesus's body on the third day after His death, they wondered how they would roll away the huge stone blocking the entrance. But when they went to the tomb, they found the stone was already rolled away, and the tomb was empty!

See, My favor will remove the stumbling blocks in your way.

With My favor, you will never need to worry; walk in obedience, and receive My rewards today.

See, there is an abundance of favor wrapped up in your obedience today.

Yes, I want to favor you even more today!

What areas of favor are you lacking?

What areas of obedience do you need to tap into?

Whatsoever measures you give will be measures given back to you also.

Your key to favor is obedience, so use it to open the door today.

My Response to Prophetic Poem 17

This has always been my constant prayer, asking, "Lord, give me favor with all I come in contact with, be it my students, my supervisors, or just about anyone else." But then I realized favor just comes from God being pleased with me being obedient.

I have decided to dig deeper and get all God has for me. The Bible shows that Joseph was endowed with God's favor. I searched the scriptures to find where he disobeyed God, and I could not any. Now I made the connection that obedience really showers us with God's favor.

PROPHETIC POEM 18

This Season Demands Worship

Worship in the store, worship in the marketplace, and worship in
the fields today as this season demands worship!
When the enemy comes to suppress your worship, press on even
more, and you won't need to retreat.

It is worship that will disappoint the enemy.
It is worship that will cause your focus to be on Me and not on
the circumstances.
It is worship that will give you the strength to continue and
overcome.
This season demands worship.

Should you feel depressed and like hope is running away from
you, get to that place of worship, so you will continue in the
race.
If you find that you are seeking newness and refreshment of
spirit, worship will allow you to dress in fine linen.
Let worship be all in all you do, and let it be first in your life
and immensely rewarded for this act of adoration to Me, God.
This season demands worship!

My Response to Prophetic Poem 18

To truly worship God is one of the highest forms of adoration to God. Worship is more than singing songs. It is how you live your life with the attitude of putting God first, above all others. This becomes evident when we seek to please God with fervent and diligent hearts.

I heard this story from a godly man who went to church one Sunday. During the entire service, he felt so miserable. After the service, he felt even more depressed and was not able to sense the refreshing presence of God. On his way home, he met a woman with her five children, who did not have a Sunday meal and other necessities. He gave them money and drove them to their destination. As soon as he did this, he felt the sweetest and most awesome presence of God surround him, and he began to weep and worship God.

What I am saying here is that we are all unique beings before God, and legalism, or our prescribed way of approaching God, does not always provide us with the answers we are seeking. We tend to fill our churches today with programs, not presence. God must remain our focus in all we do. That man was not able to fulfill the plans God had for his life if he remained committed to church programs. But someone may say we need to have order. Yes, order is a wonderful thing—as long as the Lord is not left out of the order of arrangement. Most times we think He approves of our beautiful buildings, but what He is after is our empty, aching hearts, so He can fill them with Himself. Our main focus is not to have beautiful buildings with air-conditioning, padded chairs, and people who have not been able to experience Jesus, who comes to set captives free and heal their broken hearts, as in Isaiah 61:1–3. We spend time to focus on a particular day, place, or style of worship. However, the great Almighty God cannot be placed into the little boxes we carve out for Him. It is not the right church or the right location; it is the attitude of the heart. Just like the woman at the well who spoke with Jesus. She believed God was at a special place, where her father worshipped him. But Jesus affirmed to her then and to us today that God is not at a special physical place, and we must worship Him in spirit and truth.

There will be a time when many of us will not find those beautiful buildings. Economic issues will cause some of them to disappear. Moreover, this generation is not looking for buildings or a particular day or location. They are ready to worship God wherever and whenever because if God is truly what He claims to be, worship should flow out of us naturally anytime and anyplace. I hear some people say we are not to talk about God at the workplace for we may be fired. But where is the safe zone to talk about Him? Wisdom must guide us, but as true believers, we cannot limit God to a safe zone. We have to make a conscious effort to spread His name everywhere we go and in all our actions.

PROPHETIC POEM 19

Let Me Father You Today

I want to father you today.
I want to fill that missing piece in your life.
I want to father you today.
You will never get all the things you may need, until you have
    agreed for Me to father you.
What does a father do for his child?
He loves, he guides, he protects, he corrects, he chastises, he
    rewards, he provides, he blesses, and he adores his child.
He will never let his child go without love, and that is why I say
    that I love you, and with that love, I have provided shelter
    for you.
Are you lacking in love? Seeking love and moving from one
    relationship to another, hoping to find love,
Looking for love in all the wrong places and never feeling
    fulfillment?
I want to give you the Father's love today
Where can you turn if you are hurting?
Who can you run to for assurance?
Allow the Father to provide for your needs today!

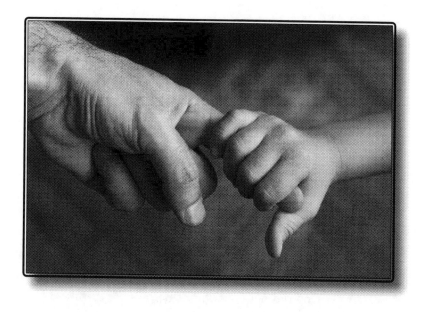

My Response to Prophetic Poem 19

I never had a relationship with my earthly father, so I never knew what it meant to be loved and cared for emotionally by one during my early years. Because you don't have a father does not exclude the desire to have one. Neither does it remove the pain and hurt. Moreover, the child who has no father figure faces fears of not being wanted or loved.

I made all the wrong choices in relationships and have spent the rest of my life living the consequences. There was a time in my life when I didn't want to even have male figures as supervisors because I fear that they were abusers. However today I have grown and matured in Christ, and that has changed. When I got to know God as my heavenly Father in a deeper way, He showed me that He was different and that I could trust Him as my Father. With this knowledge, I immediately knew that all my needs were taken care of, and I was loved and adored. I am a new person in Christ, and it is all because of the warm and loving relationship that I have with God, my Father.

Today I understand the emotional trauma for children who have no father figures because they are missing out on a whole lot in life. Until they come in contact with the heavenly Father, they will not be complete. God did not mean for us not to have earthly fathers; even Jesus had an earthly father. I want to tell the fathers who have neglected their responsibilities to pray for forgiveness now, and ask God what you can do to make it right with your children. I always searched hard for a father figure and never found one. Through the years, I have met many students who have no father figure, and one can't imagine how desperate they are at times. It is incredible to see that they can cope and wear a smile on their faces, even in the midst of their struggles.

We must be thankful for fathers for they play a special role in our lives. Let us treasure our earthly fathers and give them the respect and honor they deserve. I want to implore men to remember their roles as earthly fathers and live a life that all children who come in contact with them will gain fatherly protection and respect. We treasure and pray for our fathers, whatever capacity of life they are in, because they were placed in our lives to fulfill needs even beyond our scope of imagination. Therefore, when they fall short on doing God's best for their lives, we must seek to encourage them always.

PROPHETIC POEM 20

Again I Say Rejoice

Those perplexed and tormented souls desperately seeking peace,
rejoice, and again I say rejoice.

Those seeking rest, rejoice.

Learn to rejoice so that you may find My peace during the storm.

Rejoice in the Lord always, so your heart can be guarded, and
your spirit can be refreshed.

Again I say rejoice in the Lord always!

Rejoicing is the tunnel that allows the beautiful waters of peace
and hope to flow into your heart.

Whatever your condition may be, just rejoice today.

It is in your times of joyfulness that you gain strength and
overcome the forces of darkness.

Darkness cannot live in a heart that is filled with joy, so call your
joy to come forth now, and let heaviness disappear.

Say the joy of the Lord is your strength.

Your joy must come now and remain.

Again I say rejoice!

My Response to Prophetic Poem 20

It is important to note that depression cannot live in a body that is always praising God. This is all the medicine you will need. Depressive spirits left Saul as David the psalmist played music for him. We can't allow one day to go by without offering praises to God. Let praises begin and end our day. Do it whether you want to or not. They say the first thing a lion does in the morning when it awakens is to make a loud roar to show that it is alive. Shout praises to God. It will keep us alive. The reading of Psalm 150 is one way to start our day.

The benefits of praise are rewarding; we fight our battles by praising God. We use praise to silence the enemy as in Psalm 8:2. The interesting fact about praise is that we never want to praise God, and that is why it is called a sacrifice. When we receive the next negative report, we must condition our spirits to praise God, even when we don't want to. Victory is assured with our praise. God deserves praises for He alone is God and does marvelous things. Psalm 66:2 calls for us to "Sing forth the honor of His name and make His praise glorious."

We are often bound and held captive by the enemy, and the only thing we can do is praise God. The scripture showed us an example in Acts 16:26, when the imprisoned Paul and Silas prayed and praised God at midnight, hoping for a miracle. It must have been a difficult time for them as midnight symbolized their worst moments. But in a short while, a new day would unfold with the victory they desired. With their praise, the prison doors were opened, and they were set free.

Our midnight crisis may be the inability to sleep at night. Sing praises to God as we lie awake, and the enemy will soon flee. Or it may be other negative issues. We must come to agreement with God and follow His principles to praise Him even in our most difficult times. This brings us the freedom Jesus secured for us on the cross.

PROPHETIC POEM 21

I Say Decree that You Will Finish What You Have Started

So you fear that you have too many unfinished projects and are
    not able to finish them.
We will speak to that spirit called "unfinished projects" and
    command it to leave your life right now in Jesus's name.
I say decree that you will finish what you have started!
For whatever begun in My name will finish in My name, and
    you will finish strongly and triumphantly.
The enemy's plan was for Jesus not to come and to complete the
    plan of salvation for humankind. But Jesus persevered and
    finished strong, and so will you.
At Jesus's birth, King Herod wanted to kill Him; His earthly
    father, Joseph, was warned by an angel in a dream to escape
    to Egypt. Your plans might include possible death and appear
    they will never be realized. They will not die but spring forth
    with new life. They will live and be successful in every form
    and realm. You may need to listen for My specific leading
    and hide yourself in prayer and praise, but you will prevail.

The devil also tempted Jesus, hoping for the prophecies not to be
    fulfilled. But Jesus used the Word and overcame temptation.
    So will you. When you open your mouth and speak My
    words, there will be no match for the enemy, and he will flee.

My words in your mouth is the weapon you will use to finish strong.

You will also have to choose the path of surrender to finish strong. Your total surrender is crucial to finishing the race that is set before you.

Peter told Jesus not to go to the cross, and he had to rebuke that voice of the enemy. For the enemy will not have you surrendered. According to Jesus, "except the grain of wheat falls into the soil and dies and abide alone. But if it dies, it brings forth much fruit." (John 12:24).

Remember that whatever the enemy did to prevent Jesus from fulfilling the plans of the Father will also be done to you. But you now have the key, so use it. Jesus remained triumphant, and so will you.

Another key to finishing strong is to hide yourself in prayer. Use the Word against the enemy, and surrender every area of your life so that My plans for you can be accomplished.

Make the decision today to finish strong for there is much uncompleted work to be done.

What areas of your life need My finishing anointing?

Are they your dreams, your relationships, your children, your marriage, your family, your career? Is it your life or even your soul?

Then activate your faith today, and make the decision to finish strong.

Decree that Jesus is the Author and Finisher of your faith. Begin to activate your faith.

Decree that He who has begun a good work in you will complete it. Whatever God has started in you He will see through to the end.

Decree that your dreams shall not die but come to fruition.

Decree that you shall live and not die to declare the works of the Lord. There will be no untimely death; you will come to your grave at a full age.

Decree that you shall build houses and inhabit them, and that you shall plant vineyards and reap them. This is for those whose hard work amounts to nothing.

Decree that your children shall be as olive plants around your table.

Decree that you shall be like a tree, planted by the rivers of water, that brings forth its fruit in its season, and whatever you do shall prosper in Jesus's name, Amen!

My Response Prophetic Poem 21

What are the unfinished projects in your life today? Which areas of your life need the finishing touch of the Master? This may be your job, your marriage, your children, or just something that you have been waiting for the Lord to do for you. Those who are thinking of divorce may want God to finish what He started in you and your spouse. Say aloud that what God join together let no man put asunder (Mark 10:9). Some of us have faced the thoughts of premature death, but God will satisfy you with a long life according to His Word in Psalm 91:16. Allow God to finish what He has started in you. If you are a child of God, He has placed these dreams deep in your heart, so He will see them to their completion.

I need a daily touch from the Lord so that I can get the strength to finish strong. I can think of my job, teaching teenagers and young adults, and this is a task that requires a strength that is beyond me. One simple mistake can destroy your career. One word not fittingly spoken can be catastrophic. These precious lives have been entrusted to me for whatever reason, and I cannot fail. I must finish what God began in me. But God has always given me His word that He who has begun a good work in me will complete it (Philippians 1:6).

PROPHETIC POEM 22

You Shall Never Have Another Breech

This time you shall receive strength to bring forth
This is your season to bring forth, says the Lord.
Those dreams that have been lying dormant will now begin to
    burst forth with new life as my light is shined onto them.
What are your dreams, big or small? Let me have them for it is
    I who has given them to you.
You shall never have another breech!

Let those desires of yours come into full agreement with My will,
    and allow Me to set you ablaze with a fire within that is
    unquenchable.
Many have come to this point and failed to let God take them to
    the end of their journeys, so their dreams quickly withered
    and died.
But wait, and see that there will be no breech!

But you have received My Word, and it has fallen on good soil
    and will bear a hundredfold.
You have received My endless grace, which is sufficient to carry
    you through.
You have received My strength, which you will need to persevere,
    even in times of drought.
Watch for the season of My plans coming to full term, and no
    more breech.

This season I will cause the waters of heaven to rain on your dreams, so you will receive the desires of your heart.
Watch those dreams that I have placed in your heart for they will surely come to pass.
You shall never have another breech!

My Response to Prophetic Poem 22

Wow! "You will never have another breech," says the Lord. I felt really surprised but excited to hear the Lord say this to me. I had to research this area to understand what a breech really is, and it led me to breech birth. This is when the baby is born with the bottom first rather than the head. Today I sense that God is spiritually saying that His plans for us must come to full maturity with no hindrances. Whatever negative circumstances happened in the past will not happen again. No more breech birth!

PROPHETIC POEM 23

This Time You Will Give Birth

So you have fasted and prayed, hoping to see the day
That you will give birth.
You have wondered if this will ever happen.
Will that time ever come for you?
Will you ever behold that which you call glorious, as Simeon said
    when his eyes saw his salvation?
Just as I revealed to Simeon that he would not see death until he
    saw the Christ child, so you have been given this revelation.
But I say to you that the long struggle of barrenness is over!
What has been stolen must be returned sevenfold.
I will begin to open the places that have been closed.
As I opened the closed womb of Hannah so see she could bring
    forth, so will I open those hearts that have been closed to My
    purposes.
Begin the rejoicing as you prepare for the birthing process.
The pain will be evident, but the joy that will encompass this
    moment will be even greater.
It may appear dark now, but the light is about to burst forth,
    and the darkest part is just before dawn.

My Response to Prophetic Poem 23

Be determined in your mind to birth the plans God has for your life. It does not matter how many failures, disappointments, struggles, pains, sicknesses, grief, traumas, and abortions that have hovered over your life. All that really matters is that you have matured enough spiritually to come to the place of surrendering all to God. This plan is not really about you; it is about a great God who made you in His image and had one purpose for you: to worship Him. Therefore, let your light shine just for God.

Be ready and willing to answer the call of, who will stand in the gap? God is looking for watchman on the wall. In Ezekiel 22:30, the Word of God says that He sought for a man among them who would make up the hedge and stand in the gap before Him for the land, but He found none. We must give God permission to use us to carry out His will on the earth.

PROPHETIC POEM 24

Your Prayers

Your prayers are about to move the mountains in your life today.
Your prayers are about to give you the breakthroughs you have
    been longing for.
Your prayers commission angels to come to your deliverance
    today.
Your prayers are about to bring forth a new fragrance that is
    pleasing to God today.
Your prayers are about to see all fears disappear and a new and
    profound realm of faith stand guard in its place.
Your prayers are about to let you speak only those words that
    are pure and true, so you can call those things that are not
    as if they are.
Your prayers will ignite all those around you with a mighty glow
    that will drive away all the darkness, death, and destruction.
Your prayers are powerful for our relationship; they are what
    binds us together.
Just like Daniel, your answer will come if you just keep pursuing
    Me, knowing that God hears all prayers that come from a
    heart that safely trusts in Him.
Just like Job, your calamities will turn because you have prayed
    for those who disagree with you.
Just like David, you have poured out your whole heart before
    Me, and I am listening and working even this very hour on
    your behalf.
So keep all your prayers alive and constant as my angels collect
    them in incense and bring them before Me daily.

Pray without ceasing, pray continually, pray about everything, pray anywhere, and pray everywhere as I am listening to your requests and will make all blessings abound for you.

A life without prayer does not hold Me as first place; I want to be the first one you run to for all your answers.

The lifting of your constant prayers, even when there is no light in sight, is sure testimony that your trust is placed in God, therefore pray, pray, pray; your prayers are being answered even at this very hour.

Those provisions you believe are out of reach will now become available to you.

The prayers of the righteous prevailed.

Will you let prayer provide you with the answers you seek today?

My Response to Prophetic Poem 24

I usually pray about everything, small or big. I vividly recall how one day my refrigerator broke down when I needed it the most. We had a heavy lightning storm, and I heard it go really quiet. I went to bed the night with the freezer overly packed with perishable goods. The next morning, I woke very early to check on it, and it was still not working. I cried out to God in desperation to fix it for me. After a while, I looked it, and it was working normally again.

I have prayed over little situations and received countless miracles. I prayed over the broken car, and it worked. I prayed over my pain and was healed instantly. I prayed over my loved ones and others who were sick and watched God heal miraculously. I am not saying all this to give any attributes to myself; I have absolutely no power to make anything wholesome. The power lies in Almighty God, who I belong to. I give Him glory for all the miracles He has performed.

This is how God uses prayer. One Friday afternoon, about one year after I was saved, I was watching a soap opera, which was my usual thing to do then. Suddenly, I felt a pressing burden come upon me. I began to cry, unaware that I would soon get dreadful news. I heard the Lord's voice anxiously say, "Pray! Pray! Pray!" So I turned the television off and prayed.

Within ten minutes I received the phone call from a family member, who sounded hysterical. She told me my nephew received a sudden blow from someone. He was unconscious and being taken to the hospital as she spoke to me. My world came apart. I could feel the pain, like a sharp knife piercing my abdomen. It must have been the worst pain I had ever experienced at the time. My tears were uncontrollable as I cried to God for immediate help for this loved one, who was very close to me.

He remained in a coma for three days. The doctors were not sure if he would wake up or be normal if he did because his life-threatening injury was located above his ears. This was one of the times when I prayed and cried without ever having a meal. The wait was agonizing. After three days, I received the news that he was out of the coma, and his condition was upgraded to serious but stable. The doctors were surprised that his condition had miraculously changed for the better. I praised God like crazy for this miracle. The following Sunday, I went to church, and the choir sang "Look What the Lord Has Done." During the service, I praised God unashamedly, dancing like David did because this was a miracle from God. Today I still gave praises to God Almighty for keeping my nephew alive. It has been almost twenty years since the accident. I have not watched a soap opera since then because I want to always be on the alert.

PROPHETIC POEM 25

Let Everything that Hath Breath Praise the Lord

The only thing you need to praise the Lord is your breath!
If you have a breath, lift up mighty praise unto the God of
heaven and earth.
Say, "Let God be praised for He is good and gracious to all."

Say, "Let God be magnified for his righteousness extends to all
generations."
Say aloud, "Our God inhabits the praises of His people."
Say that "God is great, and His greatness is beyond all human
understanding."

Say, "God is not limited to time; He is outside all time. He has
no age for God does not need time. God remains changeless!"
Say, "God is not limited to space. He is bigger than the earth; the
earth cannot contain Him. His greatness is beyond measure."

When is the right time to praise Me? As long as you have breath
for the breath belongs to Me. I loan it to you for one main
reason: to praise Me. You were created to worship.
The next time you begin to think of the right time and place to
praise God, just remember all you need is your breath.
So let everything that has a breath praise the Lord!

"Make a joyful noise unto God all ye land; Sing forth the honor of his name: make his praise glorious. Say unto God how terrible art thou in thy works! Through the greatness of thy power shall thy enemies submit themselves unto thee." (Psalm 66:1–3 KJV)

My Response to Prophetic Poem 25

God gave me these words one morning when I woke up and didn't feel like praising Him. I was just tired and overwhelmed. And He said aloud in my spirit that I should let everything that hath breath praise the Lord. Remember that praise will help you to win the battles you face today. When we begin to praise the Lord, we silence the enemy or the accuser of the brethren as the scriptures records it. The enemy's power is words. He used words to tempt Jesus. They were just words, but they could have been effective if Jesus did not understand this level of warfare. The believer who is equipped will have scriptures ready for any assault of the evil one. Moreover, praise is also important to have in your mouth as a weapon.

PROPHETIC POEM 26

The Just Shall Live by Faith Says the Lord

What area of your life has heavily weighed you down today?
I say the just shall live by faith!
What problems keep occurring over and over, even after you have
    prayed, fasted, and waited?
I say the just shall live by faith!
It is a simple word, but the affect is very great as the just shall
    live by faith.

My Response to Prophetic Poem 26

I received this word in church from the Lord as I stood in prayer, crying about all my needs. The Lord responded in a sharp voice, saying, "The just shall live by faith." I cannot count how many times I have held onto faith as if my life depended on it. I remember one time when someone close to me was ill. I had seen very sign, both physical and in dreams, that she was not going to make it. I love this person more than life, and I also love her children dearly. My heart's desire is for her to live a long and healthy life. I called my church family to join me in prayer as the Bible told us to call for the elders. This close relative was a thousand miles away in another state, so I asked her permission if my church family could pray with her on speakerphone, and she said yes. We went to prayer, bombarding heaven for her. I put all I had into this prayer for about an hour. After prayer ended, I was about to go to sleep when I heard the enemy's voice, saying she would not be healed. This voice was terrifying to my ear. I felt afraid and was so weak spiritually, even after the prayers we offered up to God on her behalf. I instantly heard God's voice say, "Put your faith into this," and to stand on the words I had just prayed. The Lord's voice was enough to strengthen me. I held on to His words that night like a drowning person, trying to keep hold of a lifeline for survival. It was a hard and long night for me. I walked around my bed and decreed and pressed into my faith reserve. The next morning, I awoke, and to my surprise, she called me at around 6:30 to say she had taken her child to the bus stop for school. This is a miracle! She had not able to walk to the bus stop.

We must press into faith like never before, but God will endow you with the necessary strength. Your battles may be greater at each level, but there will be a greater level of faith. Don't worry about the storm. Expect God to give you grace and favor in every one. We are more than conquerors!

PROPHETIC POEM 27

The Angels of the Lord Encamp around You Today

Know that you are not alone as My angels encamp around you
today.

Know that you are protected from all harm and danger as My
angels encamp around you today.

Know that you are protected from the thoughts of the enemy
that may come in your mind for My angels stand guard to
keep you from falling.

Know that you will only listen and obey My voice, and not
another, as My angels encamp today.

Know that My eyes watch continually over you to keep you safe.

Know that there is a more powerful and mighty host of angels
with you than the enemy.

See for yourself that you are kept safe from the terrors by night
and horrific pestilence by day.

Know that with long life I will satisfy you, and you shall not
die before your time.

Today, even as you sleep, My angels stand guard with mounted
weapons, ready to fight on your behalf.

The next time that tormenting spirit returns to taunt you, just
know that My angels encamp around your dwelling place.

You have been assigned specific angels today that stand guard
at your door.

My Response to Prophetic Poem 27

I received this as I was doing my morning prayer. The Lord showed me that His angels are encamped around me, and the enemy could not have his way. Whatever problems you are struggling with, just remember that the enemy will not prevail. I usually remind myself that the same God who has begun a great work in me will complete it. (Philippians 1:6).

A few days before I received these words for the poem, I had a strange dream. This dream took place on a Sunday afternoon, after I returned from church. For the entire weekend, I felt sense of uneasiness in my spirit. It was as if I could sense an eerie presence of darkness, hovering about my home. However, I was too tired to even pray about it, so I took a midday nap. During this nap, I dreamed a huge man was standing with a weapon by my door. This upper part of the weapon was the size and shape of a vacuum cleaner, gray in color. The lower part appeared as a huge, gray and black gun, its nozzle resting on the floor. I did not see this extremely tall man's face, but I somehow knew he was there to protect me, to offer instant help if I needed it. When I awoke, I had one of the most peaceful and serene feeling. There was no fear, just a peaceful sensation. I didn't remember the dream until after dinner. I told it to my loved ones, and then they interpreted this to say that an angel of the Lord was standing guard at my door while I slept. I was ecstatic to know that God sent His angel to watch over me. This is the same for all who put their trust in God.

PROPHETIC POEM 28

Push through the Door, Even though It Keeps Pushing Back

Break the door down if you must, but you must enter.
Don't let anything hold you back now for you are right there at
    your place of deliverance.
The spirit of determination will arise in you as you pursue your
    difficult paths.

The enemy wants you to give up, to procrastinate, to delay; you
    must push through the door even when it keeps pushing back.
You have no choice but the choice to go on; keep moving forward
    in the Spirit.
Be relentless, be bold, be vigilant, be sober, be wise, be victorious;
    take your stand as you plant your feet firmly, using God's
    powerful words of strength.

Always believe you can do all things through Christ, who
    strengthens you.
Always believe that you are more than a conqueror.
Always believe that your latter shall be greater than the rest.
The next day will be even better than all the rest.
Always believe that you are above and not beneath.

Keep pushing forward until you enter the place of your destiny,
    your place of success, your place of promotion, your place of
    prosperity. The place where you were meant to be.
Never give up! Pursue your dreams! Go all the way!

Push through the door, even though it keeps pushing back. Keep pushing. You cannot fail. You will surmount all obstacles in your path!

Never yield to tiredness, never yield to weariness, never accept mediocrity, but, instead, persevere and enter!
This is your chance to enter. You must enter now!
Possess your promises. Possess your prosperity.
It is God's plan for you to walk through your open door, and you must give it your all.

My Response to Prophetic Poem 28

What are the assignments in your life that you know God has laid on your heart to accomplish, even in the face of difficulties? God has endowed us with His strength to accomplish every task, but we must persevere. These words are for that person who needs to be forceful and not allow passivity to rule over his or her spirit. There are some dreams our spirits know we have to accomplish, and we have no way but to push in and enter.

I vividly remember when I was about to enter teachers' college. I was turned down over the phone by the college admissions officer as there was a waiting list, and competition was tight. A career in teaching was most attractive for many young people during this time. I envisioned myself being a teacher all my childhood, and when I finally reach the age and intellect, I applied to the teachers college, hoping to pursue a career in teaching. I know I was called by God to be a teacher. Even my principal spoke this word over me that I was going to be a teacher. It was now my time to war with that prophetic word. To my surprise, my application was denied, but I was not about to take no for an answer. So I went to the college in person. As I entered the college campus, I could sense that a battle was brewing in my spirit. This dream of being a teacher was God-ordained, and nothing was going to hinder His plan for my life. I realized I had already faced lots of obstacles in my early life. Some I had no control over, such as being fatherless and lacking emotional support. However, I did the best I could and worked hard to pass all my high school exams, and, therefore, this was my moment.

I entered the huge hallways of the college, and as I approached the office, I met one of the college advisers. I handed her my high school credentials. She checked them and told me to complete an application form, pay the required tuition fees at the bank, and report to class the following Monday. I was accepted just like that!

What would have been the consequences today if I had taken no for an answer? These classes had already been in session for a week, and there was no way you could be allowed to begin the semester that late. However, there was still one big hurdle remaining. I was not able to get the tuition fees. And after much praying, God provided the funds. This is pushing through the door, even when it keeps pushing back!

You may be facing hurdles as a student with your grades, as a mother with your child in difficulties or a negative doctor report, but pray, praise, and speak the scriptures over your hurdle as you enter God's plan for your life. Since then, I have faced countless hurdles and overcome all that would have prevented God's plans. If God has placed a dream in your heart, don't allow it to die. These dreams are for eternal value as many are waiting for you to touch and transform them. Thousands of young people have crossed my path, and each day, I thank God for the privilege of having a positive impact on their lives. Some are more difficult to handle, but we are given these precious lives. We must give our very best in order for them becoming successful adults.

PROPHETIC POEM 29

It's Time to Come Home

Will you tell them for Me that it is time to come home?
They have been falling away and developing a wandering spirit,
Searching for what they will not find outside Me, God,
Growing among thorns and thistles that prick them daily.

Please tell them that it is time to come home.
It's getting late; the door is still wide open.
Tell them I am standing at the door, waiting like a father waiting
    for his prodigal son.

I am waiting, waiting, looking, looking, pleading, pleading for
    you to come home, come home, come home.
With open, outstretched arms waiting for them—My treasures,
    My treasures, My treasures, come home, come home, come
    home.

To you, My favored ones, My unfailing love for you is beyond
    human understanding.
I waited for them to come home, to enter My supply realm, My
    realm of abundance, My realm peace, and My realm joy; My
    sweet place of satisfaction.

I am speaking to My treasured ones, My unfailing ones, My
    redeemed ones, My loved ones, and My favored ones.
I remember your prayers and how you asked to get deeper with
    Me, God, and now that invitation of deep relationship has
    been extended for all to come home.

As the father saw the son far off and ran to meet him.

"And he arose and came to his father, but when he was a great way off the father saw him and had compassion and ran and fell on his neck and kissed him." (St. Luke 15:20)

My Response to Prophetic Poem 29

The urgent cry of the Father is for all to return home. While He will call and beckon us to come home, there is no guarantee that we will get all the time we need. We must make it home while there is still time. As Christians, we have completed powerful and incredible assignments for God. We have cast out demons in Jesus's name, allowing people to be at liberty; preached to millions and watched them accept Jesus as Lord and Savior; written numerous books on every necessary topic for spiritual maturity; built huge, magnificent buildings for God's worship; and planted churches in the most remote corners of the globe. But that does not guarantee that we are at home with the Father. If anyone has ears to hear, let him or her heed the Father's pleading and come home. The Prodigal Son reached a point in his life when he couldn't continue, so he made the wisest decision and returned to his Father. Heed the call now, and come home to the Father.

PROPHETIC POEM 30

Pass the Test

The test is included in the package of life.
The test makes the life package complete.
There will be no life without testing.
It is the test that makes you strong.
Pass the test!

Develop perseverance during your times of testing.
Embrace the test as this will be your time to shine.
How will you know what you are capable of accomplishing?
Everyone dreads a test, but we will never know what we can do
    until we are tested.

Tests will always be there; they will never stop, and they will be
    to the degree that you are able to pass them.
But one thing to know is that your great God will never present
    you a test that you have not been prepared for, so remain
    strong.
There is not one test you have not been able to withstand and
    come out victorious.

My grace is all-sufficient for you.
One main key to passing the test is trust.
I trust you enough to allow you to go through the test.
But will you trust Me to take you through it safely?
You may look at all your limitations, but stop and see that I can
    fill all your weaknesses with My strength.

The next test will be easier now that you understand God is in the midst of the tests and has already prepared your deliverance.

Enjoy sweet peace and rest always. I love you too much not to have you tested. You will pass them to go higher and higher in Me, God. Love to you from your abiding friend, God.

My Response to Prophetic Poem 30

I was thinking of how heavy my burden is to bear as I wrote these words in the poem. The Lord spoke to me and said the difficulties are there because He expects us to pass the test each time. He reminds me of Abraham and the many tests he went through, so we will never escape tests. Psalm 11:4 reads, "The Lord test the righteous."

What do we do when the next test comes? We just submit to God. We deliver ourselves in His hands and seek His guidance about what specific actions to take. We must be spiritually equipped for each test as they will always be coming. But God is not a grasshopper in our path; He is a great giant. Many have given up because of a test, though God knows that we are already well equipped to undergo any degree of testing.

PROPHETIC POEM 31

Nothing Missing, All Complete

I see nothing missing and all complete when I look at you.
We have nothing missing when our lives are given up to Christ.
All your good works have been recorded.
The greatest prize, or award, is for the Lord to say, "Well done,"
    at the end of your days.

Job was tested beyond human understanding. When tragedy
    struck his family, he had every reason to say something was
    incomplete, yet he said, "Thou He slay me yet will I trust
    Him" Job 13v.15 and I know that my Redeemer lives and
    He Shall stand at the latter day on the earth." Job 19v.25.
    Throughout all his pain, he kept his eyes on the Lord.

What was taken away and missing were returned to him more
    than he had before.
"So what is missing that I cannot complete?" asks the Lord.
Let the Lord be the focus. Fill your eyes with Him only, and
    whatever is missing will be of little importance. God will be
    great and be God in your life as only He can deliver.
There is nothing broken; everything is whole and all complete
    with Him.
You have My approval that My great plans for your life have
    been accomplished.
Which is to know Him, to have Him, and to love Him by just
    being obedient to His Word.

My Response to Prophetic Poem 31

Over the years, I have always dreaded the invite to family gatherings, such as Thanksgiving dinner. This is the usual time when the family gathered for more than just a meal and giving thanks to God. It was also a time to showcase our individual accomplishments. I was always fearful about attending because of my inability to have children. So hiding from family gatherings was the safest way to protect myself. The lie the enemy told me was that "It is usually at these reunions you realize how much you are incomplete, especially when everyone presents their children, and you have nothing to show." However, God was about reveal the truth that I am whole and complete with Him as my Lord and Savior.

My earnest desire is to gather with family. I would pay anything to have my own family since I never had much of one when I was growing up. I had no father; he separated from my mother as soon as I was born. But she did the very best she could under the circumstances. Over the years, I have seen many babies born into my extended family. Many born even before I got married now have their children. This sight has been an extremely embarrassing one for me.

However on this great occasion, I struggled once more with accepting this Thanksgiving invitation. A feeling of inadequacy entered my mind, and I began singing, which I usually do when I am seeking an answer from God. I then heard the Lord spoke in His stern, fatherly tone I have come to know as that familiar voice. He said, "Nothing broke, everything whole, and all complete in Him." I have His assurance that His great plans for my life are being accomplished. Which is to know Him, to have Him, and to love Him by just being obedient to His Word. I instantly knew that a supernatural healing had taken place in my heart. This was on the eve of Thanksgiving, and I immediately began shopping for Thanksgiving dinner. I was happily on my way to meet with everyone. The next day, I allowed my fears and self to die. God's words of strength became the substance that runs through my veins.

On Thanksgiving, I deliberately tried to arrive as late as possible, after all the main introductions and festivities were complete so as not to be seen or heard. But when I arrived, the welcome and love my husband and I received was so amazing, and this display of emotions must have been a miracle. I felt love and acceptance. That moment I realized my absence from family gatherings over the years had been worse for the family than for me. They want to be with us, even when we are hurting. I know I have been healed.

Make family gatherings opportunities to spend time with family. Let them know how much you appreciate them. God is all about family. He wants the family to come together in unity and the entire household to be saved. The father was not able to rest until his prodigal returned home. Keep expecting our loved ones to return to the fold. As Christians, you may not agree with their views or actions sometimes, but we have a responsibility to strive for what God desires for our families.

PROPHETIC POEM 32

Wisdom for Every Situation

I will give you wisdom for your job.
I will give you wisdom for your marriage.
I will give you wisdom for your family.
I will give you wisdom for your finances.
I will give you wisdom for your   .
I will give you wisdom for every situation.

Walk with me; seek me first about the situation always.
Each time the situation appears difficult, remember I am there
    with you.
I will give you on-the-spot wisdom; as you need it, so I will
    pour it.
Even to overflow when you need an overflow.

The fear of the Lord is the beginning of wisdom. That's all you
    need; just ask and seek after My wisdom, says the Lord, and
    it will be granted as needed.
Boldly speak life over the situation; use words of hope, peace,
    and joy.

My Response to Prophetic Poem 32

Wisdom is identifying the source of the issue and applying the unique solution to the problem without fear or other constraints. Therefore, if you lack finances, ask the Lord to give you His wisdom on this, and whatever He says to do, be obedient. Are you spending more than you earn? Are you tithing or giving to your church? These are serious issues for if you are not able to give, you will only have your little to rely on. Can God trust you with a hundred dollars? If your answer is yes, He will be able to trust you with a thousand dollars. What if you receive a thousand dollars now, how would you spend it?

Many people receive a thousand dollars first they will go shopping or pay bills. However, that is not the order in which God plans for you to spend your money. Consider this order for your money: tithing, giving offering, saving, billing, and spending. Whatever you do, put God first in all. Don't make this practice legalism, but develop a close relationship with God and His Holy Spirit through Jesus, His Son, who loves you and wants the best for your life.

I remember when I inquired of the Lord about buying a car. His response was to use wisdom. I thought about how I could use wisdom when buying a car and came up with four main criteria. First, you must be able to afford the car without buying on credit affordability). Second, it must be a strong car or a good make (durability). Third, it must have a fair resale value and not depreciate quickly. And fourth, you must like the car enough that even after two years, you will still want to keep it.

When we need wisdom, just ask God as He promised to supply our needs. Sometimes wisdom requires patience; if it sometimes leads to hasty decisions, it may not be God. Wait for the peace of God to rule over your heart. Then you will know the decision is of God.

PROPHETIC POEM 33

My Love for You

For all the things I want to say to you this day, one is that I love
you more than these words can ever say.

Let me write My banner of love over you with words that cannot
be erased but will always remind you of My insatiable love
for you.

Let Me show you how much I love you today in all the ways you
have never imagined anyone could ever love you.

Let Me visit you as I please and never leave because we were
meant to be; we are inseparable, and I love you.

Let Me keep close to you with My unbreakable bond of love for
I love you.

Let Me perfect all that concern you for I love you.

Let Me shelter you from all harm and fears for I love you.

Let Me be your strength, so you will not go weary for I love you.

What can I say to My fair one to make her embrace My love?

With an everlasting love have I always loved you.

Today, love the "Lily of the Valley" visits you and rearranges
your life with beauty and passion for I love you ever so much.

My love for you is free and unconditional, and it never requires
a reason for I just love you. I even engrave your name

on the palm of My hands and look at them always for I love you.

With My love, I have forgiven you, cleansed you, and restored you for I love you, My fair one, My child.

My Response to Prophetic Poem 33

> 'Rise up my fair one and come away for low the winter is past and the rain is over and gone. The flowers appear on the earth; the time of the singing of birds has come and the voice of the turtle is heard in our land. The fig tree put forth her green figs and the vines with the tender grapes give a good smell. Arise my love my fair one and come away'! (Songs of Solomon 2:10–13)

During the writing of this poem, an awesome sense of peace washed over me as I breathed the heavenly aroma of love. God's love is all we need to make our lives complete. Love is everything. We all search for love, want to be loved, and hope not to be disappointed. But while we may have people who show us love, they can never love us like the Father does. It was because of love that Jesus came. For someone to give his life for his friends is love. To die for humankind to have eternal life is even greater love. Think of a love that is unconditional: "Greater love has no man than a man to give his life for his friends" (John 15:13).

God expects us to extend this love to others. Don't allow our love to grow cold. Love is also something we do. Love is so complex but also very simple as each person interprets and receives love in his or her unique way. While it may just take a pat on the back for some to feel loved, it may require you to spend time with someone or give gifts. However, we must show love to each other. Always meditate on this powerful word to keep love ablaze for others. Ephesians 4:17 states, "That Christ may dwell in your hearts by faith; that ye being rooted and grounded in love."

PROPHETIC POEM 34

Is the Soul Healthy?

We worry about our present, temporary existences or the states
of our bodies, but we rarely consider the states of our souls.

Is the soul healthy? Is it safe? Is it okay?
We take our bodies to the doctor for every simple itch, but we will
miss the bigger picture if we neglect to take our souls to the
God of heaven, who made them in the first place.

Jesus tells us to possess our souls, and only the Holy Spirit can
diagnose the true state of our souls.
We can only be sure if we give it to the Lord to transform us in
His image.
This message is not only for the sinners but those who believe
they are inside the will of God when, in fact, the enemy may
have them deceived.

The lies of the enemy may appear as the truth, but truth can
only come from one place, and it is in Jesus.
Jesus speaks of some who were hypocrites, looking beautiful on the
outside in white sepultures, but inside, they were dead men's
bones.
Soul check 1,2,3; soul check 1, 2, 3; soul check 1,2,3.
Make haste now, and take your soul to the Holy Spirit, just like
we would take our bodies to the doctor.
Come in to Him. You don't need to say a word about your
condition for He knows why you come.

He sees all your faults. He knows where the stuff that corrodes our systems lie. He has the remedy.

This process may take three minutes, three hours, three days, or even months, depending on your willingness and honesty. If you hold back during this process, you are only wasting your time and deceiving yourself. You will receive nothing but will be left with more torment.

Don't be busy when you come. Have one agenda, and just quietly sit and wait at Jesus's feet.

You will know when your request is met. Your heart will know instantly. You may not have any specific feelings or emotions to reassure you, but you will know.

A serious note to all is that the soul never dies. It lives on forever, and you have the choice to decide its eternal destination. At the death of the physical body, the soul never goes into the casket. However, everyone goes somewhere, the soul to hell or heaven. Learn from Jesus. Jesus presents us an example of the rich man and Lazarus in St. Luke 16 v.19-31

God Almighty has done everything possible to deal with the soul problem. This is a real soul problem, since humankind sinned in the Garden of Eden. The penalty for sin was death. The problem of the soul arises. God made His plan B by having Jesus coming and dying on the cross. Jesus shed His blood and offered up His life for us.

Many in the church will say, "Don't we all know that?" The answer is yes, but most of us believe that we will get time to make it right and have our "soul check" done. Matthew 25 v.1-13 presents us with the parable of the ten virgins who were waiting to meet the bridegroom. They were all expected to be part of this special ceremony however only the five wise ones were able to enter. But we are never certain of that tomorrow we will have the chance to make everything right. No one knows the final moment. Moreover, this is the job of the Holy

Spirit, and He may not be there when you decide to have your soul checked.
Therefore, make the wisest and healthiest decision and have your soul check now—today!

My Response to Prophetic Poem 34

As I was writing these words, two of our friends passed. These sudden passings were unknown to me at the time of writing. However, God had a plan for these words to reach others who yet have time to hear this and act. We must understand that while we don't all have the same time on earth, we have the assurance of eternal life when we accept Jesus by believing that He died on the cross, shed His precious blood to cleanse us of sins, and confess Him with our mouth as Lord and Savior of our lives. It must be the heart cry of every born-again child of God to get as many souls as possible into the ark or to be saved. It pains my heart to know someone may not receive eternal life, and I didn't do all I could to introduce that person to Jesus.

PROPHETIC POEM 35

You Are a Success Story

You may have had a difficult life, a difficult year, or even a
difficult situation. But you are a success story.

You may have a broken relationship, broken heart, or broken
dreams, but that cannot remove My, God's words of success
written over your life today.

You may have prayed and prayed and seen no answers in sight
to your prayers. The fact you are alive in body and spirit are
all the answers and signs you may need right now to know
your life is a success.

You may even see everyone else having all the things you so
greatly desire. And you may repeat these words more than
once: "The Lord grants you the desire of your heart."

Let me reassure you that you have success in other ways, even if
you don't have the specific success you desire.

Look at your circumstances today, and see that the right hand
of God stands in your midst!

The enemy plans for disappointment has become your greatest
promotion.

The enemy meant for those horrible, painful years you had in
the past to destroy you, but God meant for those mishaps to
build you, to position you, and to promote you.

How do I know that you are a success story?

Because you meditate on God's Word always.

Because you are accomplishing God's plan for your life.

You always place God's Word above all other words, so words of failure, defeat, worry, anxiousness, and even death have no power over you.

There is an even greater level of success intercepting your path today as you pressed into the Most High God.

Which would be of greater success to you? Is it to have all the things your heart yearns desperately for and not to have Him? Or wouldn't you rather have Him and receive His peace, which is freely given?

To have God is to have a successful life! No other paths guarantee success.

Your words of success are heard.

Your success is determined by Him, God, not by personal gain, property, or power.

The greatest success is to know Him, to have Him, and to enjoy the promise of everlasting life with Him.

Your life is a success story! God is all the success we need. Our restless hearts will not find true and lasting peace without Him.

My Response to Prophetic Poem 35

The world's definition of success varies according to people's particular interests. If you ask students what success means to them, they will say to pass all their classes and tests and eventually go to college. If you ask the teacher, he or she may say to have a smooth school year. The world's idea of success is having enough money to afford all the luxuries of life, and to be happy and healthy.

This is to say success means different things based on your expectations. However, this is not God's definition of success. It is not measured in how much money or how many material goods we have, or even how healthy we may be. Instead, it is defined by accomplishing God's plans for your life. To ensure success, we must seek after God before all other things. The scriptures urge us to "Seek ye first the kingdom of God and His righteousness and all other things shall be added unto you" (Matthew 6:33). To have success or a favorable report in all things, small or big, we must first go to God to hear what He has to say on the matter. Whenever we have a negative doctor's report, sudden bad news, or in making any decisions, even in relationships, if we ask God, we will surely get an answer. Sometimes we must be patient. However, the peace of God will be in your heart, so you will know what to do. Joshua 1:8 says the Bible's blueprint for success is to meditate on the Word of God.

PROPHETIC POEM 36

Asking, Seeking, Waiting for a Sign

Many have been asking, seeking, and waiting for a sign from
heaven.
They ask, "When will God intervene on the earth and put an end
to the disparity, deprivation, destitution, and the destructive
forces hovering over the lives of people?"

But the only sign I will show is the sign of My coming back to
earth.
The sign of My unending mercies and My amazing grace,
blanketing the textured mountains like snow; this is the
amazing sign you will see.

The sign of miracles and my healing power will cause the sick
to be healed, diseases to disappear, and captives to be set free.
Many will even see the dead rise and come to new life. That
will be an incredible but true sign for all to see.

Lost ones coming to salvation by the droves, hundredfold, and
by the ten-thousands fold as they receive My redeeming love
will be a beautiful sign for the world to see!

Old men seeing visions and young men dreaming dreams as
my Spirit is poured upon the earth all over again will be a
glorious sign to behold!

Not the sign of chaos and confusion, not even death and destruction, as many will point to. But a new life of abundance and My mighty working power over My people spreading forth as a hen covers her chicks will be the sign the Prince of Peace is returning to gather His precious ones.

The dove, gracefully spreading her wings of My presence over all who will receive, causing human hearts to sing for joy, will bring a settled peace and assurance of hope. This is the sure sign of My coming.

The sign of the light, magnificently lay out like millions of shooting stars, lighting up the darkest midnight sky is the great sign you will see.

This light will shine everywhere, from the obscurities of the cities to the great halls of fame and palaces, and all will see the marvelous signs of My coming.

The signs are everywhere in hearts and souls now as My coming draws nearer and nearer (Joel 2:28 says "And it shall come to pass afterward, that I will pour out my spirit upon all flesh, and your sons and your daughters shall prophesy, your old men shall dreams dreams, and your young men shall see visions."

My Response to Prophetic Poem 36

At the end of this prophetic poem, I said wow! I was not expecting the Lord to present all these positive and marvelous signs to show His coming but, rather, to look at all the negativity around us as true signs of His return. The wars and earthquakes that Jesus spoke of are also signs that the end is near. I believe that God wants us to focus on the positive, expect the positive, and see ourselves growing deeper each day with Him. We are not naïve; we are aware of the destructive forces present in our world today more than ever. We have seen powerful earthquakes kill hundreds of people more than once. We have seen many Christians beheaded for their faith in Jesus, and we hear disturbing threats of chemical warfare. Therefore, we are all aware of the disasters, both natural and human-made, that hover over our planet.

But God is still in the midst, and the fact is that we are alive at this time for a great purpose: to be used by God. The questions that we need to ask ourselves are, How will we perceive those signs? What are our roles as Christians during this time? What preparations are we making to get our lives ready for the harvest that is coming? What if today was our last day on earth; how would we spend it?

PROPHETIC POEM 37

Prepare for the New

Prepare for the new! Prepare for the new! Prepare for the new!
To overtake new territories, to trod new paths, to sing new songs,
to devise new tactics, to receive new mantles, and to ride new
waves in the Spirit.
This is not like anything you have ever seen before, and it will
baffle even the wisest. Signs of the new will spring forth
everywhere, like a gigantic burst of sweet-smelling fragrances
filling the atmosphere.
Many will say, "Let us taste that which is pleasant to our
spiritual senses."
A new boldness will embolden you to speak the truth with
authority and expose the lies and deceitful practices that
have been told to My people.
No more will they accept good as evil and evil as good, but they
will be able to discern for themselves every evil occurrence
hanging around.

There will be new voices arising in the worship of adoration and
praise to God ascending to the throne room, causing you to
join the angels singing in the heavenly choir. So loud will be
the new sounds that even those who are spiritually asleep will
be awakened and dressed up in fine garments.

New nations birthing forth sons and daughters to carry the
mantle of salvation, shouting, "Grace, grace, and grace," to
the impossible.

New movements in the spirit realm will uproot the generational curses of the cycles of lack and neglect holding My people captive. Placing them in the place of abundance and position to receive all they need.

New zeal and passion to continue in the race and reach the finishing line, knowing that He who began a good work in you will see that you accomplish all tasks set before you.

Tell My people it is the new that they have never seen before.
The new, like the day when the ark of the Lord emerged from the land of the Philistines, and David danced uncontrollably and unashamedly before the Lord for the person, power, and presence of the Lord has arrived!

My Response to Prophetic Poem 37

The words of this poem entered my spirit like the bolts of lightning. I was burning on the inside. As I was getting dressed for work early one morning, I felt this sensation of power, joy, and victory bubbling with great excitement inside me. I really don't know how to explain this. I had never felt this great force of power, peace, and freedom in such a way. I began to prophesy loudly the words, and I wrote "Prophetic Poem 37." I knew that I was giving birth to the supernatural. I had been filled with the Holy Ghost ten years to date, but this was more intense and fire hot. This is an experience I really don't know how to explain except to say that I was free at last. My prayers were answered! I was giving birth to the supernatural. I was giving birth to something huge, which was the climax of what the poems were all about. This feeling lasted for an entire day. When I arrived at work, I wanted to shout for joy all day. But I still had a physical job to do. This one moment changed my heart forever. It was like I have tasted of Him.

While the world is rapidly changing with new technological gadgets or innovations in health, medical science, and astronomy, we also envision that the spiritual world is also changing. God and His Word never change. He remains constant, though we humans change. There is so much about God that we have never seen or experienced before. We must prepare for the things that God is doing momentarily, or we will miss out on Him. Each time God shows us another side of His goodness and mercy, we are changed in His awesome and majestic presence. This is not what we have done; it is all because of a great and all-powerful God, who is marvelous in all His ways. We praise You, Lord God. There is none like unto You, and You alone are great!

We must prepare for what coming in this season. When we prepare, we hold an expectation of something about to happen, we remove our old garments, we change our old mind-sets, we get cleaned up and dressed up for it, we keep our lamps filled with oil; we are always on fire. God does not have to remain in the little boxes we made for Him. That is why we must go after God with a passion now more than ever. Do not be blindsided by the materialism of this world, by shopping, by the news reports, by engaging in useless toils. Make our lives count for eternity. Do only the things of eternal value. Time is short, and the toil is long. Laborers are urgently needed in the fields. Will we go for God?

PROPHETIC POEM 38

Take a Sure Stand

Take a sure stand, and plant your feet on the path where I
place you.

Allow nothing to remove you; many will see that you are
unmovable and steadfast in all your doings.

In doing so, you will take a sure stand against all opponents and
naysayers who have said you will never amount to anything.

For all words spoken against you, will and have already come to
naught, and all deeds done to you will not go unnoticed for
I, the Lord, is with you always, helping you to take a sure
stand today.

Decree that your path will grow brighter and brighter, while the
path of the unjust will become darker and darker.

Decree that the there is a sure place where you can hide and
where no fowl know and the fiercest of lions have not walked.

Decree that the captive exile is hastened and may not die in
the pit.

Take a sure stand, and plant your feet on the sacred paths that
I have purposed for you to walk.

Worry not about what adversities may try to befall you as you
have already come through your fiercest storms.

The storms that were meant to take you out have propelled you
to go further along the journey.

You have now gained new strength to plant your feet in the firm
foundation.

This time, nothing shall disturb your peace for you have taken a sure stand.

You shall be like a tree planted by the rivers of water that brings forth its fruit in its season, and its leaves also shall not wither; whatever it does shall prosper.

They who trust in the Lord shall be as Mount Zion that cannot be removed but abide forever.

My Response to Prophetic Poem 38

If you have lost your confidence in the tumultuous waves that have swept your path in the last season, this is the time to get back in the Word of God and develop confidence and strength to go the next part of the journey. Most times when we hear unfavorable reports we get sidetracked. As humans, we stop to think of the roles we need to play in every situation. However, we are on a journey and cannot give in to every report we hear. But it is time to begin to sink our minds deep into what God's purpose is for us and keep moving.

PROPHETIC POEM 39

Will You Say Yes?

Will you say yes today to my plans, the plans of God?
Many lives are embedded in your yes, in your obedience, in your
answering the call of Who will go for Me, God?
Will you say yes to the plans that I have implanted deep within
your spirit today?

The plans that I destined for you to walk in even before the
foundations of the earth.
Even when it is shrouded in difficult circumstances, like Esther
had to endure; even when it will cost you your life, like Paul
who was shipwrecked, beaten, and later, his eventual death.
Will you say yes?

Likewise, Moses ran away from Egypt and refused to return to the
very place where I intended to make My glory manifested by
the showing of mighty signs and wonders in the outpouring
of pestilences to release my people from bondages and slavery
in Egypt.
Even when it does not seem to make sense in the natural, will
you say yes?

Will you say yes today to My plans?
Many lives are embedded in your yes, in your obedience, in your
answering the call of, Who will go for God?
Many lost souls are hopeless and waiting for your prayers to
sustain them or transform them.

It was the same plans that I had planted deep inside Abraham
when he was asked to leave his father and journey to start
a world with new ideas built upon God's Word. These ideas
continue today and will throughout eternity. Abraham said
yes, and the results today—and forever—are as innumerable
as grains of sand on the beach. Will you say yes?

This was the plan God had for the saving of a nation by a
young girl named Esther. The Jewish people in Persia faced
the onslaught of a demonic regime. But Esther, the epitome
of My love for humankind said yes to My plans. She placed
her pleasures in second place and made My plans to be first.
She came to the palace for such a time as this and vowed to
carry out God's plan, even in the face of death.
Will you say yes?

Will you say yes to go even beyond the journey, beyond the call,
like Elisha who pursued Elijah for that double portion?
Will you say yes to birth the answers the world is seeking, like
Mary said yes and gave birth to the Savior, and eternal life
is made possible for all by the blood of Jesus?
I am waiting for you to say yes. Will you say yes?

Will you say yes today to My plans, God's plans?
Many lives are embedded in your yes, in your obedience, in your
answering the call of, Who will go for God?
All it takes to say yes is an agreement bond that is sealed by My
Holy Spirit and thus, a separation from the things of the
world. Remember, you are in this world but not of this world.

All it takes to say yes is My Word to enter and dwell there, like a
seed planted that grew into a beautiful and fruitful tree for
many to partake of and be filled.

All it takes to say yes is your determination to say, "I will go on, even if it costs me everything." For your yes will cost you everything. But what will be gained is even greater.

That you will not look at your imperfections but will look at your Maker makes all things perfect.

That you will not look at your circumstances but will see that God is bigger than any obstacles in your path.

That you may not listen to the naysayers or those who think the task is not of God, but you will know in whom you believe and trust that it is best to please God than man.

Say yes today, and see that all your efforts will be rewarded. Your yes to God will be the answer to millions waiting desperately to be released from captivity. Love them enough, and say yes to Me today.

Sometimes, the very places, faces, and circumstances that we don't want to face are the exact plans God has for our lives. That's the spot where He wants us to work for Him and for His glory to be manifested.

Don't hide like Adam did, don't run like Jonah, don't complain like Jeremiah, don't deny Him like Peter, and don't look at your limitations like Moses. Be like Caleb, who said, "Give me that mountain." Be like Mary, who said, "Be it unto me Lord as your will," and the Savior of the world was born! Just say yes. Heaven will record your obedience when you say yes to My plans.

My Response to Prophetic Poem 39

Saying yes to God is actually saying no to self. It is that total surrender of self and allowing God to have full control. Each time we choose not to surrender, we have to go around the mountain again, which is a waste of time for our spiritual growth. The same issues we have last year should not be present this year. If they are, we have the power to overcome. The power of fasting can break these recurring issues, whatever they may be.

There was a time in my life when I struggled with a particular issue, and I fasted and prayed all day. At the end of the fast, I was terrified by this same recurring issue even more than before. I cried out to the Lord, and I heard the Lord say, "Now you have the power to act." I commanded whatever was bothering me to leave my life in Jesus's name, and praise God, that thing never returned to taunt me.

PROPHETIC POEM 40

Be Encouraged, Always

I want you to be encouraged today by knowing that you are
not defined by the difficulties you face. You are not defined
by the mountains that stand in your way or the recurring
issues that will not go away even after you have prayed many
fervent prayers.

You are defined by God's faithfulness and your persistent
perseverance and determination that always keep you
encouraged. This is a sure testimony to keep memorizing
that you are forever and safely kept by the power of God's
amazing grace.

The difficulties you face today are your stepping-stones to
a victorious road, paved with God's goodness and mercy.
Therefore, you are encouraged in this dire situation.
Take this journey called life with hope as the rising of the morning
sun because you will always get your chance to shine brightly,
even when dark rain clouds linger vehemently overhead.

The sun never refuses to shine at its best; even when you
don't see it, the sun remains a full, powerful force, shining
magnificently as if to light the hearts and souls of those who
have fainted in spirit and body and need to be encouraged
with God's Word.

Take the Word of God as that instant medicine, and push it into
your soul, bones, and marrow to revitalize you as you need
that strength to stay encouraged always.

"God is not a man that he should lie; neither the son
of man that he should repent. Hath he say it and
shall he not do it hath he spoken and shall he not
make it good."(Numbers 23:19 KJV)

God hears us when we call on Him, will answer our every request,
and will never ignore our pleas for help.

Therefore, be encouraged with the mind-set that you are not
lying down but running to win every race before you. Don't
whine and cringe under the heavy burdens; God has already
prepared the victory. Be encouraged as if you know the
answers have arrived.

David encouraged himself in the Lord when his dearest
possessions—his two wives—were taken away from him. And
while his heart was overwhelmed with despair, he decided to
encourage himself in the Lord by asking for direction.
The direction you seek may be the same one given to David—to
pursue the enemy and recover all.
Whatever the Lord places on your heart as the answer, it will be
just what you need to overcome and recover.
I speak a new volt of life into whatever has been dead or dormant
in your life today so that by the power of the Almighty God
and in the name of Jesus, you will be encouraged and rise up
with a fire burning in your path, strikingly evident for all
to see and realize that you are not retreating.

This time, you must go after and recover all; this is the
encouragement that you need, that all is well in with you and

your loved ones, and whatever else you hold dear in Jesus's name. Shine today like the morning sun for your brightest days are about to unfold!
Be encouraged.

My Response to Prophetic Poem 40

There will always be tests and trials because that is how we really grow and show maturity in God. So don't give up when things don't go the way you planned. You must keep going on; keep pressing into God. When you feel faint, and your strength gets weak, know that God has all the strength you need. "He gives power to the faint and to them that have no might He increased strength" (Isaiah 40:29). "The Lord is the Strength of my life" (Psalm 27:1b). We must purpose our hearts to continue on the journey of life. Don't falter by the wayside; keep pressing on.

I once heard there are two main ways that lions catch sheep: when the fire goes down, they come to take the sheep, and when the sheep lags behind and does not walk with the other sheep. Do as the Word commands and speak to yourself in hymns, songs, and scriptures. Just keep the fire blazing in your soul.

And do not be alone spiritually and physically. When I say spiritually, I mean that you must remain in constant fellowship with God daily. Don't make this legalism, such as reading five or six chapters of the Bible each day, showing your efforts. Instead, develop a relationship with your Father God. Practice His presence around you, and learn to hear His voice in your daily tasks. If you don't hear Him, trust that He says He will never leave or forsake you. Physically, have sisters and brothers in Christ to guide you. Find time to meet with them in study groups, and study the Word always. The key is not to allow your fire to go cold and the Holy Spirit not able to dwell with you because of sins not confessed. Always run to God, not away from Him. There will always be tests and challenges. Sometimes, you will feel like it is the worst time of your life, and you may never recover. However, the plans God has for you are ones of peace and an unexpected end. Isaiah 29:11 and 1 Corinthians 10:13 say that "there hath no temptation taken you such as is common to man, but

God is faithful who will not suffer you to be tempted above that he is able, but with the temptation also make a way to escape that he may be able to bear it."

God's main purpose for us is to possess the land. When He took the children out of Egypt, His goal for them was to possess the land. His goal has not changed. We have a job to do; we must keep fighting and expect to win for we are more than conquerors. Let our fires keep blazing for God.

MY PRAYER TO THE
GOD OF MY LIFE

Dear God, I must tell You this. I really want to tell You that You have made my life complete. I don't have a need that You are not able to supply for You are there to fill every void in my life. You are there to erase every urge that displeases You. You are all I could ever hope for in a friend and a Father. You watch my every move and listen to my every sigh, making sure that I dwell in peace and safety. So let me say this is my prayer to the God of my life.

This day I want to tell You that I am so thrilled to have You as my greatest supporter. All the times I needed a hand—and a very big hand—to lift me up, You have held out Yours for me to hold. You have continued to hold out Your hand, even when my stubborn self needs lots of reassurance. I will always say this prayer to the God of my life.

I have been through the dumps, I have been through the pits, and I have been by the wayside. You never left me there. You drew me out to a place of safety and protection. You brought me out of a horrible pit and miry clay, set my feet upon a rock, and established my goings. When I faced rejection and needed a friend to turn to, You showed up and offered me Your friendship. Even when I faced betrayal, with hurt tagging along by my side for a season, You came and spoke words so caring, so precious, and so comforting that I received Your instant peace. That's why I say this prayer to the God of my life.

Every time I see myself, I am looking at a miracle, and a big miracle, too. Countless times You have sent your angels to rescue me from death and place me back on the path of life. You have given Your angels charge over me to keep me safe always. When I am in pain, it never lasts; pain loses its power over me as soon as I run into Your forever-healing presence. When I choose to worry, Your still voice reminds me to take no thought for what tomorrow may bring. You are the God who holds tomorrow, and not me. What a God You are to me. Words are not adequate to describe you, oh, great Adonai. I want to say this prayer to the God of my life.

This day I will write the story of my life, the story of success, the story of peace, the story of deliverance, the story of forgiveness. The story's headline is that I am washed in Jesus's blood, that I am an overcomer, and that I am more than a conqueror. This story will be told to all who will listen.

You are the God who enters my life and rearranges it to suit Your grand purposes and plans. Your plans for me are to accomplish more and more, to bear fruit, to have peace and prosperity, and to see my cup overflow with Your goodness. To win every battle as the battle is always Yours.

You show me symbols and signs in my dreams, speaking to me all night during my sleep, giving me instructions. As soon as I am awake, Your words entrap me and invite me into that place so secure and so secret to spend the day, to spend a lifetime. I gladly accept. Then You speak to me, using Your calm and loving voice to tell me You love me. I am mesmerized. I am in love with You and Your presence. I want to keep beholding Your glory. I cry out to You, "Lord, show me your glory," and you do.

I wait for You at times to give me answers, but sometimes you say trust is the fruit that You hope to develop in me. You said to trust You even when I don't see the way forward. I tried, and sometimes it is difficult. But You always help me to make it over the mountain, so this prayer is said am to thank the God of my life.

I will say thank You, Lord, for guiding me to a place of power over the little foxes that seek to rob my peace. When I didn't know how to fight, You placed the sword in my hand and filled my mouth with Your powerful words to trample on the path of the destroyer and gain the victory. This is my testimony and prayer to the God of my life.

I ask for forgiveness of the sins of fear, doubt, anger, worry, jealousy, resentfulness, and _____. May they never find a safe home in me to dwell as this is my prayer to the God of my life.

I want to ask You to help me to be myself and not someone else, so I can carry out Your plan for my life.

I will say to my friends, my family, all unfamiliar faces, and even my foes that the God of my life will never disappoint you. You will never ask and not receive of Him. He is always a giver, the giver of my life, the giver of health, the giver of all good and perfect things. What are your needs, big or small? May they be aligned with His plans for you. While you wait patiently to watch, the God of my life fulfilled them. Please give Him your life and your time, and watch Him rebrand you just for Himself.

This day, I am indebted to You for the great price You paid for my salvation through Your Son, Jesus. I pray that many will come to faith in You and taste and see that You are good, and Your goodness endures to all generations. You will wipe away their tears, even the ones they hide and no one knows. But You see their pains and hurts. You will turn their mourning into joy and remove their fears, so they can be bold to speak Your name, even if it costs them.

This prayer is to the God of my life. The God who hears when I call and always gives me the strength and will to soar like an eagle.

Lord, let this prayer touch the hearts of whoever may read it so that they can, in turn, touch other hurting hearts with Your love. Thank You for loving me, Lord.

I sense an awesome feeling of satisfaction that I have indeed accomplished what God set out for me to do. I knelt to pray when I sensed the poems must end with a prayer. This prayer depicts my relationship with the Lord and how He has possessed my reins continually, according to David in Psalm 139:13: "For thou has possess my reins and has covered me in my mothers womb." At the end of this book the Lord has impressed upon my heart that "His secrets are with them that feared Him and He will show them His covenant" Psalm 24 v. 14.

God wants us to realize that He has many secrets to impart upon those who truly seek hard after Him. This seeking after God is not a physical work but a spiritual resting or surrendering of our will so God can do His work in and through us. The central theme of this book is to show that God wants to be first place in our lives. God wants us to live for His purpose only! Give God first place and let Him reveal to you His secrets that will transform you daily into His image.

04167862-00967312

Printed in the United States
By Bookmasters